CONTENTS

PREFACE

For many years I have been greatly impressed by the many excellent articles in *The Wall Street Journal* which examine, describe, and discuss various aspects of labor relations. These articles, which deal with a variety of current topics and recent developments, are extremely well written and treat their subject in a way that is relevant, interesting, and useful to those who would like to learn more about this subject. As a consequence, I have long been convinced that the best of these articles should be made available to students in the form of an inexpensive publication. This book of readings is the result of that conviction.

Labor relations essentially involves the employer's relationship with one or more labor unions that represent his employees. Of course, the nature and character of a labor-management relationship are affected by many factors such as the state of the economy, the characteristics of the industry, the management of the organization, as well as developments in labor law and legislation. However, this book is primarily concerned with the two most important ingredients of labor relations: (1) labor unions and labor leaders, and (2) collective bargaining, including not only contract negotiations but also grievance handling and arbitration.

The primary purpose of this book is to provide supplementary readings for undergraduate and graduate students taking such courses as introduction to or principles of labor relations, labor economics, collective bargaining, and personnel management. Therefore, the book is organized in a way that tends to parallel the discussion of labor relations found in most textbooks: the first section of the book consists of sixteen articles which deal with labor organizations and their leaders, and the second section contains nineteen selections which discuss various aspects of collective bargaining.

Many of the articles can be used not only as supplementary readings but also as case studies; as such, they provide an excellent opportunity for classroom discussion of a variety of issues dealing with unions and collective bargaining. As a consequence, this book can also be utilized profitably in non-credit industrial and labor relations courses for supervisors, managers, as well as union officials.

My appreciation goes to Mr. William Beardsley and Mr. Peter Sprague of Dow Jones & Co. for their help, encouragement, and cooperation in the preparation of this book. In addition, I am grateful to my colleagues Dr. Joseph F. Byrnes and Professor Carl F. Nawoj for their valuable suggestions.

Karl O. Mann
Rider College

I. LABOR UNIONS AND LABOR LEADERS

The labor movement is one of the most powerful and influential institutions in the United States. With a membership of almost twenty-two million, unions have a tremendous impact on almost all aspects of our existence. Through collective bargaining, they greatly affect the decisions made by both profit and non-profit organizations; through their political power, they often influence the election and actions of federal, state, and local government officials; and, through their economic power, they have become a major factor in the economic life of virtually every man, woman, and child.

However, the tremendous increase in union membership and power that characterized the 1930's and 1940's has not continued in more recent decades. As indicated by the first article in this section, "State of the Unions," the American labor movement today is struggling to maintain its relative position of strength. What has caused this situation? Why is union membership increasing so slowly these days? There are obviously a number of explanations for this development. One major reason is the elimination of many union jobs due to the tendency of business and industry to mechanize and automate their operations; a second cause is the proportionate increase of technical, professional, and managerial employees as well as women workers who have generally been less interested in joining labor organizations; and a third explanation involves the well-known shift within the economy from manufacturing to service industries which employ mostly white-collar workers and are much more difficult to unionize. Another reason consists of disputes between unions such as the one described in "Struggle in the Fields," the second article in this section. Furthermore, public opinion has been adversely affected by the fact that, over the years, quite a few labor organizations and their leaders have been charged with improper or undemocratic behavior. For instance, "Embattled Giant" explains why one local union president was accused of mismanaging his union and "Wearing Many Hats" describes how a number of union leaders have become rich by juggling many jobs. On the other hand, however, it should be pointed out that many labor organizations and their leaders have made a real effort to become less autocratic and more responsive to the wishes of their membership as is illustrated in the article "The UMW Tries a Bit of Democracy."

Labor unions are of course continuing their traditional efforts to organize workers. For instance, "Unions and Health Care" shows that, as a result of a recent amendment to the National Labor Relations Act, unions are expected to launch a major drive to organize employees of nonprofit hospitals. In recent years, as the articles "Organization Drive" and "Hospital Militants" point out, labor unions have also been successful in organizing engineers and other professional employees who, in the past had little or no interest in such affiliation. And the article "Rocking the Boat" illustrates the fact that the organizing efforts of unions often meet considerable resistance from employees and, in some cases, even the community.

Most labor unions do not limit their activities to organizing workers and collective bargaining with employers. Thus, labor organizations frequently are engaged in political activities which seek to increase their influence in federal, state, and local governments. For example, "Unions and Politics" describes how the International Association of Machinists has supported various candidates for political office. Some labor unions have also been very much involved with social causes as is illustrated by "UAW: 'Causes' vs. Bread and Butter;" this article discusses the conflict between those in the United Automobile Workers union who strongly favor social activism and those who don't.

To a large extent, of course, the future of the labor movement is determined by its leadership. Who are these men? What do they do and what do they believe? Why are they powerful? The remaining articles in this section shed some light on these questions. For instance, "Labor's Durable King of the Hill" describes the power and influence of George Meany who, as president of the AFL-CIO, is the top union leader in the United States. However, because Mr. Meany is now about 80 years old, there has been considerable talk about his retirement; "Labor's Future" is a 1972 article that discusses a number of possible successors as well as some of the likely consequences of a leadership change. Frequently, local union leaders are also quite powerful, much more than is sometimes realized. One example is Fran Sonsini, the business agent of a local union of bricklayers, whose activities are detailed in "An Iron Hand;" another is Ray Anderson, the young and militant president of a steelworkers local, whose attitudes and views are described in "Talking Tough." And then there is Joe Molony who has been a union official for several decades; he has now retired and, as is indicated in ". . . and Joe Molony Remembers the Picket Lines," is now able to view the past, present, and future of the American labor movement in a way few others can.

STATE OF THE UNIONS

By JAMES C. HYATT
Staff Reporter of THE WALL STREET JOURNAL

The nation's unions are organizing more workers—and enjoying it less.

Just ask the United Auto Workers. The union found Ford Motor Co. management particularly resistant when it recently sought to sign up a mere seven clerks at an Alabama aluminum-casting plant. The reason for resistance: The seven clerks were salaried employes, among whom the UAW barely has a toehold at Ford.

Before the Feb. 28 representation election. "Ford flew two personnel officers from the 'glass house' (headquarters) in Dearborn to talk to each of the clerks and argue against the drive," recalls Douglas Fraser, the UAW vice president who heads the union's white-collar organizing.

And after the workers voted for the union 5-2, the company asked the National Labor Relations Board to refuse to certify the results, alleging the UAW illegally waived initiation fees for the new members. The board's regional office threw out the complaint this week.

The management's reaction to this and earlier efforts to organize salaried workers helps explain why the UAW represents only about 35 of Ford's salaried workers after years of effort. (The union has also had difficulties organizing salaried workers at GM, but it has made much deeper inroads among white-collar workers at Chrysler.)

Adding to Problems

Moreover, even though the union won in Alabama, the company's high-level appeal indicates how seriously company managements take union organizing these days, adding to the problems that organizers already face

Some problems are external: the labor-force shift into service jobs and areas where unions aren't so common; the zero organizing potential in sluggish, dying or rapidly automating industries; the fact that many younger workers know little about unions and are often skeptical of organizers' claims.

Other problems are internal: waste of unions' resources in competition for new members; lack of union funds to conduct effective organizing or unwillingness to spend available dollars.

In recent months, all these problems have been complicated by the slowing economy. In slack times nowadays, unorganized workers become less militant and are "thankful to have any kind of job," one union man says. And when union workers are laid off, unions have less dues money to spend on organizing.

Unpromising Record

Whatever the reasons, the recent record is distinctly unpromising for organized labor:

—Unions took part in more representation elections—8,916—and won a smaller percentage—only 52.1%—in the year ended last June 30 than in any year since the National Labor Relations Board began keeping score almost 40 years ago

—In that same period, the total "no-union" votes edged out total pro-union votes by 224,975 to 220,769.

—Moreover, the union batting average has continued to slump. From October through December, employes chose unions to represent them in only 49% of the 2,170

NLRB-conducted elections. In December alone, the share was 45.8%.

—The number of decertification elections conducted by the NLRB to determine if union representation should be ended has roughly doubled in recent years. The latest tally shows unions losing about seven out of 10 such elections. (All decertification elections, however, involve only a tiny fraction of the organized work force.)

—Though organized labor's strength in the U.S. has never been larger, its share of the work force isn't growing. The latest Labor Department survey found that in 1972 membership in 117 unions and 35 professional and state-employe associations reached 21.6 million, up about one million from 1968 levels. But in the same period, the labor force rose by seven million to almost 89 million. As a result, the percentage of the labor force in unions actually fell slightly, to 24.3% from 25.2%. Twenty years ago, organized workers represented about 35% of the total.

Tougher Every Day

Such basic facts and figures aren't comforting to unions. Neither are certain individual frustrations encountered in recent years. The Retail Clerks International Association has failed six times in 15 years to organize workers in the Peoples Drug Stores chain in the Washington, D.C., area. For a decade the Textile Workers Union has fought endless battles with J. P. Stevens & Co. in seeking to organize millworkers.

Surveying the general situation, Textile Workers organizer Paul Swaity told the AFL-CIO's last convention that organizing is "getting tougher every day." And some union leaders put the proposition even more grimly.

"If the labor movement keeps on the path we've been on for the last 20 years, the next 20 will be a disaster," says Joseph A. Beirne, president of the Communications Workers. Jerry Wurf, president of the fast-growing State, County and Municipal Employes Union, agrees. "Too little is being done," he says. "Many workers have never been asked to join a union."

Not all union men are so gloomy. Statistics on organized labor's share of the work force are an "improper measurement," says Elmer Chatak, organizing director for the United Steelworkers of America; he explains that such ineligibles as managers, small businessmen, doctors and attorneys should be excluded from the base. He says the labor movement consistently adds several hundred thousands members a year—

"a substantial figure in my judgment."

Mr. Chatak's own union, with over one million members, added more than 27,000 last year. In February the Steelworkers organized the 2,200 employes at a General Electric Co. appliance plant in Columbia, Md.; two years ago, three other unions had failed to organize the plant.

And the Amalgamated Clothing Workers in February won recognition by Farah Manufacturing Co., the El Paso pants maker, after a 2½-year struggle that included a boycott of Farah products. That victory, AFL-CIO President George Meany said, "will give new impetus to efforts to organize nonunion workers."

Still, few union leaders deny they need to try harder. And some unions are doing just that.

The Carpenters Union, alarmed by the growth of nonunion employment in the building trades, recently launched "Operation CHOP" (for Coordinated Housing Organizing Program). The target: the half million nonunion carpenters working in the housing industry.

The union plans to raise at least $10 million a year for organizing by assessing members up to 10 cents for each hour worked. To ease recruiting, locals may reduce initiation fees and waive penalties for former members rejoining the union.

The Steelworkers union "has more major campaigns under way now than any time since 1968," says Mr. Chatak, and it's expanding outside the steel industry. ("The Steelworkers are trying to make themselves into a conglomerate," says one wary official of another big industrial union.) The Steelworkers union already represents employes of two banks located in steel country.

The Teamsters union, largest in the land, has named Secretary-Treasurer Murray W. Miller to be its first director of organization at the national level; previously its organizing had been done at local and regional levels. "We'll spend what it takes to do the job," Mr. Miller says, in target areas including airlines, warehousing concerns and grocery chains. He has hired five field organizers.

A New AFL-CIO Department

And the AFL-CIO is beefing up its organizing activities into a new department of organization and field services. In recent years, the federation has largely left organizing to its union affiliates reflecting George Meany's belief that the unions should meet their own recruiting needs. Some AFL-CIO organizing efforts in the 1960s proved unproductive and expensive, costing about $138 for each newly organized member; at that rate, the federation has estimated, it would take $2 billion to double the AFL-CIO's membership.

There have been dramatic exceptions to the AFL-CIO's recent attitude, of course. The federation has strongly backed some organizing campaigns that have taken on the trappings of social causes. Its support of the boycott against Farah Manufacturing helped the clothing workers win company recognition. And last year the AFL-CIO raised $1.6 million to support striking members of Cesar Chavez's United Farm Workers Union after its contracts with grape growers expired and the Teamsters union signed new pacts with them. But both these campaigns were special cases; they became broad movements to aid Spanish-speaking Americans.

As the Teamsters-UFW battle indicates, union rivalries often drain organizing resources that might be more effectively used elsewhere. Such battling is particularly fierce in the public-employe sector, where much of recent union growth has occurred. One veteran organizer compares this strife to the Alaskan gold rush. "When they struck gold in the Klondike," he says, "all sorts of people got off their tails and got themselves a dog sled."

Prosperity Helps Organizations

"We have in recent months found ourselves in representation elections involving a dozen or more AFL-CIO unions as well as the Teamsters and other independent organizations," Mr. Wurf notes, "We have fared reasonably well in these elections, but we think that the resources of all these organizations could be better spent by working together to organize the unorganized."

Economic conditions also influence organizing. If NLRB figures are any guide, prosperity enhances organizing. Unions had their best recent average in 1966, when they won 62% of the representation elections; that year, unemployment was a scant 3.8%. In such times, it is reasoned, workers are less afraid they'll be unable to get other work if an organizing drive fails.

The opposite appears true in a business slowdown. Most organizers agree a worker's fear of losing a job is the best anti-union protection an employer can have. "The biggest obstacle we have to overcome is fear," Mr. Chatak asserts. "The employer capitalizes on it."

Still, some organizers insist that if inflation accompanies a slump, organizing prospects improve. If bread gets to be $1 a loaf, "big business is going to emotionalize the workers to join unions," says Nicholas Zonarich, organizing director for the AFL-CIO's industrial union department.

More Sophisticated Bosses

Some union men theorize that organizing tends to be more difficult these days because today's typical worker is less interested in unions and less informed about the benefits of union membership. Organizers face "a generation who never knew, never cared what unions were all about," says Mr. Beirne. Mr. Zonarich fears many workers "don't understand what a union means."

Furthermore, organizers find employers more sophisticated nowadays in heading off unions. Some nonunion companies keep pay and benefits close to union-bargained levels. "The ink isn't dry on I. W. Abel's Steelworker contract with the industry when some nonunion companies in the steel industry match it," says one union official. Other firms make their new plants small so that management can keep in close touch with employes and avoid the aggravations that can lead to an organizing drive.

Still other companies have used procedures of the National Labor Relations Board to delay decisions and thwart organizing, union men charge. The NLRB "doesn't conduct hearings," one union official insists. "It holds autopsies." Mr. Miller of the Teamsters says that "NLRB red tape destroys a lot of union activities. You can be stalled up there two or three years." An NLRB administrative law judge recently criticized Farah Manufacturing for conducting "a broad-gauged anti-union campaign consisting of glaring and repeated violations" of the National Labor Relations Act and acting as if "there were no act, no board and no Ten Commandments."

STRUGGLE IN THE FIELDS

By WILLIAM WONG
Staff Reporter of THE WALL STREET JOURNAL

COACHELLA, Calif. — In this dusty little town in the heart of grape-growing country, breakfast sometimes isn't a very healthy way to start the day.

One recent morning this reporter and the Rev. John Bank, a 33-year-old priest and official of the United Farm Workers (UFW) union, sat eating breakfast at a local restaurant when a dozen burly members of the International Brotherhood of Teamsters ambled in. The atmosphere, at first jovial, became more hostile as the Teamsters and the slender priest traded jibes. Suddenly, a husky Teamster approached Father Bank, hit him in the face and broke his nose. The Teamster is awaiting trial on a misdemeanor battery charge.

The incident dramatizes the explosive dispute between the Teamsters and Cesar Chavez's UFW over representation of the state's 250,000 farm workers, now in a showdown stage here in the Coachella Valley, 130 miles east of Los Angeles. Before it is over, the struggle may decide the fate of Mr. Chavez's union. Thus, the outcome is likely to have wide-ranging impact on the chaotic farm labor situation in California—the top crop-producing state—and the nation as a whole.

Rampant Defections

High-level efforts to reach an accommodation are being pressed by both sides. Teamsters President Frank Fitzsimmons conferred for over five hours Tuesday night with AFL-CIO President George Meany, who is backing the Chavez union. Nothing concrete developed at that meeting, labor sources report. In any event, some insiders question how effectively a truce between the two labor leaders could be enforced in the vineyards, where emotions won't necessarily be tempered by soothing words from Washington.

After his stunning success three years ago organizing farm workers, many of whom are migratory, Mr. Chavez has seen his power base crumble while the Teamsters—and, some say, the growers—have seized the upper hand. The defections began two months ago, when growers here in the Coachella Valley spurned Mr. Chavez at contract renewal time and signed instead with the Teamsters. Since then, Mr. Chavez estimates the UFW has lost about 150 of 190 contracts in the state to the Teamsters, and the UFW's dues-paying membership has shrunk to 10,000 from 40,000 in the same period.

Never one to take a defeat lying down, Mr. Chavez has called for a strike and a new nationwide grape boycott. His strategy is to apply enough economic pressure on valley growers now, at the height of the grape harvest, so they'll renounce the Teamster contracts and sign once again with the UFW. If this happens, the UFW hopes it may prompt the state's big table-grape growers in Delano, about 125 miles north of Los Angeles, to renew their UFW contracts, which expire in late July.

If Delano growers should sign with the Teamsters, it would be a shattering blow for Mr. Chavez's movement, whose strength has centered on table-grape contracts. Whatever happens, Mr. Chavez has vowed to fight on. Even an anti-Chavez grower admits, "Mr. Chavez will be a viable force in the labor movement as long as he chooses to be."

Midway through the six-week harvest, the impact of the strike is still hard to assess. UFW pickets—not all of them farm workers—have numbered anywhere from 800 to 1,100, but growers say they haven't had difficulty recruiting labor or shipping crops on schedule. A U.S. Department of Agriculture official confirms the harvest is running at about the same pace it did a year ago.

Melees in the Fields

Although growers are receiving about $7.50 to $8.00 per 22-pound box of grapes, or about the same price they got last year, slowdown tactics by UFW sympathizers in the field helped contribute to the 75-cent-per-box increase in this season's costs, growers say.

To counteract the picketing, the Teamsters are paying beefy "guards" $67.50 a day to "protect the workers in the field," according to a spokesman. It was one of these guards who hit Father Bank.

Tensions have risen with each passing week. There have been a number of arrests, and last week hundreds of Teamster guards and UFW pickets clashed in what the Riverside County Sheriff's office called a "mad melee of fights and beatings all over the fields." In recent days, a Sheriff's spokesman says, "there has been considerably more aggressiveness on the part of the Teamsters."

The story of how the UFW's 1970 grape victories eventually turned sour is riddled with angry rhetoric and charges and counter-charges on all sides. But the roots of the dispute go back many years and stem from the exclusion of farm workers from the original National Labor Relations Act, which provides collective bargaining procedures for industry. Although growers, Teamsters and the UFW say they favor some legal protection for farm workers, the three groups differ about the form such law should take. The American Farm Bureau Federation, a large grower's organization, wants to ban secondary boycotts and harvest-time strikes—both favorite Chavez tactics. The Teamsters favor farm-worker coverage under the National Labor Relations Act, a plan Mr. Chavez opposes because the act also bans secondary boycotts.

A Conspiracy Theory

The UFW claims the current struggle stems from a long-standing "conspiracy" on the part of big growers and the Teamsters, the nation's biggest union, to destroy the small farm workers union. Mr. Chavez considers the contracts the Teamsters signed with Salinas lettuce growers shortly after the UFW 1970 grape triumphs were announced as a "stab in the back." As evidence of collusion, the UFW officials are fond of pointing to an affidavit filed by an official of a large commercial farming concern charging that Salinas lettuce growers actively sought Teamsters representation for their workers—without asking the workers.

The UFW is also unhappy with signs that the Teamsters and the American Farm Bureau Federation have recently reconciled their once-sizable differences. Teamsters President Fitzsimmons was invited to address the Farm Bureau's convention last December, and he called for an alliance of labor and agriculture "when that alliance works for the mutual benefit of the farm worker and his employers." He closed the speech by telling the growers, "If you believe you have a grievance, let's sit down and talk it over."

The conspiracy theory is endorsed by the AFL-CIO, with whom the UFW is affiliated. Mr. Meany's strong support of the Chavez union has placed the prestige of the 13.5 million-member labor federation squarely up against the 2.4 million-member Teamsters, who were tossed out of the AFL-CIO in 1957 on corruption charges. Mr. Meany has termed Teamster activity among farm workers "union busting" and has given the UFW $1.6 million to help sustain the strike.

The Teamsters deny charges of conspiracy and contend they started organizing in Coachella Valley only after the workers themselves petitioned for the big union's representation. The UFW, however, maintains that some of the reported 4,200 names on the petitions were obtained by "fraud, coercion or deceit."

Moreover, the Teamsters claim they have long been interested in organizing farm workers, because field strikes directly affect the jobs of drivers and cannery workers, whom they already represent. Also, they say, mechanization is shrinking processing-plant jobs and forcing workers into the fields. "The more organized we are," says a spokesman, "the better we can service our members from an economic standpoint." The UFW argues that until 1970, when the Chavez movement made its gains, the Teamsters had only one contract covering field workers.

A Costly Contract

The growers also deny there is a conspiracy, and as evidence, point out that the Teamsters pact will drive their costs up about 25% the first year. They blame UFW administrative blunders and Mr. Chavez himself for losing the grape contracts. "I think he blew it," says David Smith, an attorney for growers of half the valley's grape crop. Pointing out that Mr. Chavez had all the major table-grape growers in the state on two- or three-year contracts, he adds, "If his workers had been happy and his people had managed their union in a business-like way, there's no way in the world another union could have taken the workers away from him." And, while praising Mr. Chavez for his "inspirational leadership," Lionel Steinberg, one of two Coachella Valley growers to renew with the UFW, complains the labor leader is a "very poor administrator and an inflexible negotiator." In Mr. Steinberg's view, local UFW officials are often "more interested in social revolution and agrarian reform than in assuming the normal role of union business agent negotiating between management and labor."

But according to the UFW, the real reason the growers oppose the union is its "hiring halls"—a concept that changes the traditional agricultural power relationships. Under the hiring hall system, workers are dispatched to growers on a seniority basis, rather than through foremen who, before the halls were set up, often extracted fees from both employers and workers.

Growers contend it is actually the workers who object to hiring halls, because the system splits up family working units by sending some family members to one farm and others to a different farm. The UFW concedes this happens, but emphasizes the importance of seniority rights so that jobs can be stabilized. "Without seniority, there isn't a union," Mr. Chavez says.

Moreover, the UFW claims that some foremen, loyal to growers, sabotage the hiring hall procedure in order to embarrass the union. One favorite ploy, Mr. Chavez claims, works like this: A grower asks his foremen to place a request at the hiring hall for, say, 200 workers. In fact, the foremen request only 150. When the 151st worker comes to the hall for a job, the union tells him all jobs are filled. Then the worker goes to the foremen, who tell him jobs are still available.

Up to now, the workers themselves haven't had a voice in determining who represents them. Mr. Chavez has called for a secret ballot election and predicts 90% of the workers would vote for the UFW. And many of the state's retailers, who are major targets of the UFW's boycotts, placed full-page ads in California newspapers calling for a secret ballot.

The Teamsters, however, don't see the necessity of elections at this time. As one official says, "When we believe the workers are supporting us, we see no reason for getting involved in a long, drawn-out procedure for elections."

EMBATTLED GIANT

By Norman Pearlstine
Staff Reporter of The Wall Street Journal

LOS ANGELES — Joseph T. DeSilva has been one of the American labor movement's genuine giants for 35 years.

A cocky, often dictatorial man, he has almost single-handedly built Local 770 of the Retail Clerks International Association into a powerful, 25,000-member organization that now clearly dominates the other eight Southern California Retail Clerks locals. And, while he has never been an international officer, there are many who think of the 650,000-member international as "Joe DeSilva's union" because he has so consistently scored impressive victories for the union at the bargaining table.

Through the years Mr. DeSilva has been an outspoken maverick who has often disagreed with much of organized labor. But he has nonetheless been admired by other union leaders because his programs have been so successful. He advocated and struck for equal rights and opportunities for women and blacks and other minority groups throughout the 1940s—long before it was fashionable for labor leaders to do so. And he became best known for pioneering the negotiation of extensive fringe benefits, including dental, psychiatric and predictive medicine programs for his members.

But these achievements are all history. There are those in the union and elsewhere who now think the 68-year-old leader has outlived his usefulness and should give up control. Moreover, they charge that his interest in health benefits has grown in recent years into a near obsession with exotic medical cures and that this interest has caused him to lose touch with the real needs of his members.

Allegations of Improprieties

These critics include three longtime officers of the local who have been Mr. DeSilva's closest associates for at least 20 years. The three officers of the local—Lois McKinstry, Hugo Morris and Marilyn H. Grace—have recently filed formal charges against Mr. DeSilva with the local, alleging mismanagement of union funds and other improprieties. And last week James T. Housewright, international president, quietly moved to strip Mr. DeSilva, who is paid $64,000 a year, of power and to place Local 770 under temporary trusteeship.

Mr. DeSilva says the charges against him are groundless and that he is the victim of a conspiracy led by Mr. Housewright to remove him as a power in the union. He has forcefully resisted the moves against him. He has barred the three dissident officers from the local's headquarters. He has, at least temporarily, succeeded in blocking the international's efforts to get a court order removing him from power. He has prevented 40 international representatives from taking over his office by meeting them at the door with an equally impressive assemblage of beefy business agents loyal to him.

Mr. Housewright has convened a five-man trial board to hear the charges against Mr. DeSilva. A federal judge here has set a hearing for Nov. 20 on the international's petition to put the local into trusteeship.

Some of the charges against Mr. DeSilva, which have been kept secret but which have been obtained by this newspaper, read like the routine charges that dissidents anywhere might bring against entrenched union officials: That he negotiated substandard contracts with small food markets that reduce thousands of workers' wages. That he used union attorneys for expensive personal matters. That he forced the local to buy real estate he owned and wanted to unload. That he spent union funds for personal entertainment—"such as almost daily dinners with local union female staff members."

Megavitamin Therapy

But there are other, equally serious, charges that relate to Mr. DeSilva's use of union money and other resources to support his interest in controversial health programs such as megavitamin therapy, or the use of massive vitamin doses—far in excess of minimum daily requirements—to treat mental and other illnesses. Among other things, the dissidents charge that Mr. DeSilva spends at least 50% of his time on matters "totally unrelated" to the local union, such as "meetings and correspondence with various psychological, biochemical and medical practitioners, and advising patients" on what kinds of vitamins and medicines they should be taking.

They also allege that he has spent union money for books and vitamins that aren't related to union programs. And they charge that he spends $1,150 of union funds a week on a television program that is used primarily to advance his medical theories.

In addition, the dissidents charge that Mr. DeSilva's interest in medicine and health programs has adversely affected his ability as a bargainer. They allege, for example, that in the last round of negotiations he sought, unsuccessfully, to provide podiatry, Christian Science and chiropractic care for people in the union's medical programs in exchange for a reduction in premium payments for night work for all employes. The dissidents charge that the night premium payments cost employers 10 times as much as inclusion of podiatrists, Christian Science practitioners and chiropractors in the medical program would have.

Mr. DeSilva's critics say that these actions, together with his allegedly "generally erratic behavior" show that he should no longer control the union. One of his detractors complains that Mr. DeSilva has insisted on getting copies of all interoffice memos and on giving personal approval to all letters mailed from the union. Another charges that the last round of negotiations was severely hampered because Mr. DeSilva wouldn't delegate authority even though he was recuperating from an apparent heart attack and couldn't participate fully in the negotiations.

"Sharper Than Ever"

Mr. DeSilva is quick to agree that he has a passionate, almost evangelical interest in megavitamin therapy and other health programs. A strict vegetarian, he takes five grams of niacin and six grams of vitamin C daily. (The National Academy of Sciences Food and Nutrition Board has established that the "daily dietary allowance" for a man Mr. DeSilva's age is 14 milligrams of niacin and 60 milligrams of vitamin C. A milligram is one-thousandth of a gram.) At his insistence, the local's health and education department sells a full range of high-potency vitamins and books on megavitamins and their use in the cure of schizophrenia and a host of other illnesses.

In a recent interview, he told how he became interested in megavitamin therapy in 1967 after "someone very close to me was diagnosed as an all-but-hopeless schizophrenic."

Mr. DeSilva says this person was "in and out of hospitals for months and there was no cure in sight until I ran into a book which changed her and my life called 'The Biochemistry of Mental Disease.' " That book spoke about the use of heavy doses of niacin to cure mental illness. Mr. DeSilva says he began taking niacin himself and that after five weeks "my mind was sharper than it ever was." He says he then began giving it to the woman who had been diagnosed as a schizophrenic. He says that in a matter of weeks she was completely cured.

Since discovering this use of niacin, Mr. DeSilva has lectured extensively on megavitamins and has chaired two symposiums on their use. But while he acknowledges this great interest in megavitamins and other health and medical cures, he denies that he spends more than a small fraction of his time on such activities. Moreover, he asserts that the pursuit of this interest is consistent with his duty as a union leader to look after the health, safety and welfare of his members.

Mr. DeSilva and his supporters also deny any mismanagement of union funds or other improprieties by him. "Almost every cent that Joe has ever spent was approved by the local's executive board. And McKinstry, Morris and Grace are all members of that board," one DeSilva supporter says.

Criticisms at Convention

In a suit filed in federal court in Los Angeles Mr. DeSilva alleges that the real reason the dissidents brought the charges against him is that Mr. Housewright and Thomas Whaley, an international vice president and director of the union's Southwestern division, promised them control of the local if they did so.

Mr. DeSilva is known to feel that Mr. Housewright is trying to remove him from power because he actively opposed Mr. Housewright's successful bid for the union presidency in 1968. He says that he frequently upset the international president at this summer's Retail Clerks convention in Honolulu by criticizing him from the floor. Mr. DeSilva protested a dues increase for members and adoption of a constitutional provision requiring union officials to retire at age 65. (Mr. DeSilva has since filed a $2 million damage suit against the international, also in federal court here, charging that the mandatory retirement provision unlawfully discriminates against him.) And he angrily opposed the union's endorsement of Sen. George McGovern for President. Mr. DeSilva later personally endorsed President Nixon.

The international has imposed a "gag" rule on Mr. DeSilva and the three dissidents who brought the charges against him which prevents them from discussing their fight with the press. But the three have insisted privately to friends that Mr. Housewright had nothing to do with their decision and that there is no conspiracy with him or other international officials to oust Mr. DeSilva. They have told many of their friends that "our only mistake has been covering for Joe as long as we have." Neither Mr. Housewright nor any other international officers would comment on Mr. DeSilva's conspiracy charge.

Although this is the first time that the international has tried to take control of Local 770, it isn't the first time that Mr. DeSilva has clashed with other labor leaders or with the courts.

In 1947, for example, he called Dave Beck the former Teamster leader, the "number one strikebreaker of America" after Mr. Beck refused to give Teamster support to a strike Mr. DeSilva was leading in Los Angeles. In 1948 he spent three days in jail for contempt after violating a court order prohibiting picketing of a store he was trying to organize. In the 1950s he was involved in extensive litigation with Los Angeles food employers over retroactive payment of night, Sunday and holiday premium pay. That case finally went to the U.S. Supreme Court, which in 1956 awarded Local 770 $10 million in back pay.

Mr. DeSilva, the son of a sweat-shop worker, was born on New York's Lower East Side in 1904. He grew up there and in Italy and didn't move to California until the late 1920s, when, after hearing that Rudolph Valentino had died, he packed his bags and headed for Hollywood, where he hoped to replace the movie idol.

Series of Rejections

After a series of rejections by major studios, he began taking odd jobs and finally found himself working in the produce business. By 1937 he had become a $75 a week buyer for a grocery chain, but he was fired after trying to form a union of his fellow employes. The firing led him to form, with seven other men, the union that was to become Local 770.

In 1949 Mr. DeSilva negotiated the first extensive medical program for members of the local. That program was improved during the 1950s, and in 1959 Mr. DeSilva led a strike that resulted in implementation of dental and psychiatric plans for his members.

Through all of the years he has been in power, Mr. DeSilva has boasted the strong support of his 25,000 member local. In the last local election, he got 90% of the vote running against a candidate who criticized his strong views on health and medical programs. And he claims that a vote of the membership today would show that it still stands solidly behind him.

WEARING MANY HATS

By JERRY LANDAUER
Staff Reporter of THE WALL STREET JOURNAL

Bernard G. Rubin can't remove a tumor or write a brilliant legal brief or invent a better widget. Yet he's earning about $130,000 a year, and he enjoys a $50,000 expense account. He is one of a growing breed of labor bosses across the country who juggle two, three or even four or five union jobs—all at the same time.

Only a handful of the workers he leads in three Florida counties know how Mr. Rubin beats the high cost of living. He draws $21,600 as business manager of Miami Local 478, Laborers International Union of North America, AFL-CIO. He also gets $51,167 as president of Laborers Local 666 in Miami Beach, $51,167 more as president of the Laborers Southeast Florida District Council and $5,000 to $6,000 a year as a special representative of the parent union.

Gerre Rubin, his wife, supplements the family income. She's the executive secretary of Mr. Rubin's Local 666, and she's the secretary-organizer of Mr. Rubin's district council. Her two salaries total $29,606, pushing the couple's annual income close to $160,000, not counting $1,000 a week in expenses ($49,398 last year) or a free car or a host of other valuable fringe benefits; when the 48-year-old Mr. Rubin retires he'll collect three union pensions, and his wife is piling up eligibility for two pensions more.

"I'm always busy, always running around, 24 hours a day," Mr. Rubin says, eager to curtail a telephone interview. "You'll find I'm not at all unusual in the labor movement."

Ignorance or Unconcern

Mr. Rubin appears to be right. An informal, incomplete sampling indicates that hundreds of union executives in the U.S. now hold two or more jobs and draw two or more salaries, sometimes totaling over $100,000 a year. (AFL-CIO President George Meany, the nation's top labor leader, holds only one paid union job and gets just under $75,000.) Though it's hard to document the growth of this breed, it's noteworthy that many belong to the younger generation of union leaders.

Colleagues in the labor movement generally express ignorance or unconcern about the multiple-job, multiple-pay trend; public reports to the government don't necessarily show total earnings. But a few union men question whether union officers can really handle more than one job at a time. And the AFL-CIO holds that a union officer shouldn't take extra pay for certain services closely connected with his regular duties.

Regardless of anyone's misgivings, young Jackie Presser is building an unusually lucrative labor empire in Ohio, one even more rewarding than the one established by his father, William Presser. The elder Presser, a Teamsters boss, holds three union jobs worth $65,000 a year. Son Jackie already collects five paychecks from three different unions, a job-juggling feat that yielded income of $185,000 in 1972, not counting allowances or expense money.

Mr. Presser the younger is the $12,000-a-year financial secretary of Cleveland Local 19, Bakery and Confectionery Workers International Union of America, AFL-CIO. He is the $19,500-a-year president of Local 10, Hotel and Restaurant Employees and Bartenders International Union, AFL-CIO. He gets $1,100 as recording secretary of Teamsters Joint Council 41 and $29,000 a year (plus an allowance of $6,500) as a Teamsters organizer, and he's also secretary-treasurer of Teamsters Local 507.

A Burst of Self-Denial

From Local 507 Mr. Presser received $123,981 last year, while its president, Harold Friedman (also the $50,000-a-year vice president of Bakery Local 19) got $122,881. Both men enjoyed a noteworthy fringe benefit that's being eyed by some labor leaders elsewhere.

Mr. Presser and Mr. Friedman organized the Teamsters local just seven years ago, and neither man drew any pay at first. But in 1969, when Mr. Presser was earning $36,400, the fledgling local's leaders farsightedly set up a severance-pay plan for themselves financed by union dues. Then, in 1972, when Mr. Presser's salary had jumped to $57,200, the beneficiaries dissolved the severance-pay fund and transferred the money not back to the union treasury but to themselves as "deferred compensation."

Higher-ups in Mr. Presser's unions seem unaware of all his richly rewarding jobs or unconcerned as to whether he can carry three union banners without bumping into loyalty-dividing conflicts of interest. "We have no qualms as long as the individual is doing a good job," says Graydon E. Tetrick, executive vice president of the Bakery Workers. "Concerned? How can I be concerned?" asks Robert L. Diefenbach, secretary-treasurer of the big Hotel Employes Union. "It's news to me."

Mr. Presser is either too busy or too wary to return a reporter's phone calls about his activities, but it's known he is organizing a new Teamsters affiliate, Cleveland Local 796. Success will mean yet another salary, putting him on a par with Irving Horowitz, a Brooklyn labor baron who pulls pay from six sources without having to step beyond union headquarters.

Five Locals, One Address

Mr. Horowitz heads the International Production Service and Sales Employes, a 20,000-member union that isn't international at all. Only one of its six locals occupies an outpost beyond 100 Livingston Street; five locals share that Brooklyn address with the parent union. Last year the international union reported dues income of $262,618, of which the officers took $210,640 in salaries, besides taking supplements from all five locals, too.

Mr. Horowitz received $45,725 as international president, to which he added $33,350 for service on the executive boards of the five locals. His income from each local, $6,670, exceeds the annual take-home pay of many dues payers. "We're rather closely knit," explains Robert Rao, the $24,000-a-year international general secretary, who gets a total of $14,500 more from the five locals. "By serving on the executive boards we can feel the pulse of the union."

Can a retiring pulse-taker collect a pension from each local as well as from the international? "That's a very cute question," Mr. Rao says, hanging up on an inquiring reporter. Nor will retired Recording Secretary Jack Grey provide the answer. "I absolutely refuse!" Mr. Grey shouts. In his last year on the job, the union's 12-month reporting period between March 1, 1971 and February 29, 1972, Mr. Grey got $19,975, plus $5,244 from each of three locals, $4,769 from the fourth and $4,389 from the fifth.

In theory, of course, a union can't keep dues payers in the dark about the leaders' pay. The federal government requires labor organizations to file annual financial reports detailing all disbursements to officers and employes. But a candidate for union office or an incumbent seeking a raise needn't disclose how many other paychecks he's banking, either from another layer of the same union or from another union.

Accordingly, a longshoreman wanting to tote up the salary and allowances of Fred R. Field Jr. ($54,612) must rummage hit-or-miss in Labor Department files if he doesn't know that Mr. Field is an organizer for the International Longshoremen's Association, a member of the Atlantic Coast District, president of the New York Council and secretary-treasurer of Local 856. A similarly nosy member of the Service Employes International Union would have to know that W. J. Butler is president of Local 200 in Syracuse, president of Joint Council 23, trustee of a pension fund and a member of the international union's executive board.

What's more, union reports to the Labor Department can mislead, even if the curious dues payer knows where to look. For example, Bernard Rubin's identical salaries from the Miami Laborers local and from the district council could be more than coincidence; a worker looking at the twin $51,167 figures (up from a twin $39,433 in 1971) might assume that Mr. Rubin is getting paid only once, and members of the Brooklyn union led by Messrs. Horowitz and Rao could believe that each man is getting one salary supplement instead of five. "Maybe the law ought to require reporting of a man's total salary in one central place," a Labor Department official suggests.

In fact, existing reporting procedures enable multiple job holders to gain substantial pay boosts without incurring scrutiny from President Nixon's wage controllers. One technique is to take pay for duties once done free. Until last year Karl Rogers was getting $36,300 as president of Teamsters Local 541 in Kansas City plus $7,800 from Joint Council 56. He also held a third job, as unsalaried trustee of the Missouri-Kansas Teamsters Conference. Last year, Mr. Rogers got a raise from the local and a new paycheck from the conference. His extra income: $9,185.

Rare in Industrial Unions

Such practices, it should be noted, seem rare in industrial unions like the Steelworkers, Machinists and Auto Workers. In certain others, relatively modest single salaries still prevail (Peter Bommarito, president of the 215,-000-member Rubber Workers, gets by on $25,-000). And some ranking officers freely work two jobs for one paycheck; Louis Stulberg, the $36,400-a-year president of the International Ladies' Garment Workers, serves the union as unpaid secretary-treasurer.

Men lower on the labor ladder cite practical objections to multiple jobs. "I don't know how I could ever manage," says Sigard Lucassen, who gave up being business agent of Carpenters Local 2550 in Red Bank, N.J., to go on the parent union's payroll. "It would take a Houdini to handle both jobs, and besides, the union won't allow it," Mr. Lucassen says. "A business agent should be in or around his local on a pretty continual basis."

The AFL-CIO favors one limit on multiple pay: No union officer receiving full-time pay should take extra money for managing the union's pension or welfare funds, according to the federation's code of ethical practices. "Such service should be regarded as one of the functions expected to be performed by him in the normal course of his duties and not as an extra function requiring further compensation," the code says. Yet the AFL-CIO imposes no ethical restraints (and there aren't any legal prohibitions) against multiple pay for overlapping or even essentially similar jobs within the same union.

The many-layered structure of unions in the building, maritime and certain other trades almost invites labor chieftains to collect simultaneously from the parent union's network of locals, joint boards, districts, state conferences and regional councils. And in some unions, two jobs alone suffice to put a labor leader in the $100,000 bracket.

Three-Job Houdinis

Joseph H. Seymour of the International Union of Operating Engineers draws $60,000 as business manager of several locals in Los Angeles and $23,477 as a vice president of the parent union; in 1972 Mr. Seymour also got $5,710 in expense money plus $27,350 in allowances, a benefit intended to cover unreimbursed expenses. Joseph Spingola of the Laborers draws $92,320 in salary alone—$61,120 as president of Chicago Local 1001 and $31,200 from the Chicago district council.

Three-job Houdinis enjoying five- or six-figure pay seem particularly prevalent among the Teamsters. Salvatore Provenzano, the union's boss in New Jersey, gets $52,300 from Local 560 in Union City, $12,000 from Joint Council 73 and $30,000 plus an allowance of $5,145 as 10th vice president of the international union. Boot-wearing Roy Williams, 13th vice president, has four reasons for happiness: $40,345 in salary and allowances from the parent union, $39,900 from Local 41 in Kansas City, $11,925 from Joint Council 56 and a jury verdict dismissing government embezzlement charges against him. "It seems I don't have much time for myself these days," the busy Teamster says.

Chicago Teamster Louis Pieck lacks a vice presidency, yet he already receives six figures in pay and allowances; from Local 705, Mr. Pieck got $77,468, supplemented by $9,500 from Joint Council 25 and $10,800 as a trustee of the international union; allowances totaled $4,905.

Teamster executives down the line live well, too, in part because their independent union isn't subject to the AFL-CIO stricture against salaried welfare work.

Abe Gordon, $26,500-a-year president of Local 805 in Manhattan, gets $16,000 for operating the local's welfare fund plus $16,000 for running its pension fund. "It's practically one fund, run out of one office," Mr. Gordon says, explaining how he can administer both without special strain.

Not far away in the same part of New York City, the Patsy Crapanzano family pulls down $130,000 or so a year from Teamsters Local 27. Mr. Crapanzano is secretary-treasurer of the local, trustee of Joint Council 16 and administrator of the local's welfare plan. Wife Marie, recording secretary of the local, is a trustee of the welfare fund, a job requiring her to keep an eye on administrator Patsy. Son Robert, president of the local, is another welfare fund trustee, and son Patrick, business agent of the local, is the third.

THE UMW TRIES A BIT OF DEMOCRACY

By Bob Arnold

PITTSBURGH—Like an ingenue involved in her first love affair, the new reform administration of United Mine Workers President Arnold Miller went into its first constitutional convention here somewhat naive and a little reckless.

By the time the two-week-long affair ended earlier this month, the Miller regime had lost much of its innocence. It had made some major mistakes and obviously has a lot of maturing to do before it challenges the coal operators in next year's negotiations.

But, with all that, the convention's achievements were considerable. After years of John L. Lewis' iron hand and Tony Boyle's machinations, the meeting undoubtedly was the most democratic in the UMW's history. Every delegate was given his say until the majority voted to close debate. Moreover, the union's constitution was completely rewritten, establishing the autonomy of district and local unions that previous UMW leaders had usurped. And controls were established to keep these bodies in line.

After long debate, the delegates also did away with the cause of much recent union corruption by sanctioning steps Mr. Miller already had taken to dilute the voting strength of the union's 81,000 pensioners, fully 40% of the UMW electorate. In past elections, under other administrations, retirees were alternately bribed and threatened with loss of their pensions unless they supported incumbent union officers.

The delegates also insured rank and file input into formulating bargaining demands. And they created a system for rank and file approval of industry-wide pacts, the first time in UMW history miners will have had that privilege.

On another front, Mr. Miller won the right to move the union's headquarters to a coalfield site somewhere between Charleston, W. Va. and Pittsburgh from Washington, where he said, "If you're heisted and don't have $40, they shoot you."

Some Miller Failures

But the Miller administration's failures also were notable and could have long-lasting effects. Mr. Miller was unable to push through a revision in the contract between the union and the coal industry which would have streamlined the procedure for settling work grievances and thus help stem the rising number of wildcat strikes. The union, in fact, had initiated talks on the revision and the industry had agreed to a compromise proposal last month. But the delegates voted it down.

And, except in District 20 which comprises Alabama, Mr. Miller failed to dissipate blocks of opposition in many of the districts which voted for then-incumbent W. A. (Tony) Boyle in last year's court-ordered UMW election. Surprisingly, Mr. Miller found less than total support from areas that previously had backed him in the union election—western Pennsylvania and Ohio.

Moreover, in his zeal to demonstrate his administration's much publicized democracy, the UMW leader often demurred from speaking out on the floor for issues he favored. And his own followers, many attending their first convention and unschooled in open-meeting tactics, neglected to support such issues at opportune moments. Thus an administration-backed strike fund proposal failed by a handful of votes.

Complete freedom of speech reigned on the convention floor and when a delegate didn't understand a point he usually stepped to the nearest floor microphone to ask about it. The first day ended when a delegate shouted, "We fellas down here are getting awful thirsty watching you fellas up there drink water all day. We want some water." The next day there was water for the delegates as well as in pitchers on the rostrum. Disconcerted by the disorder, the convention's planners frequently held all-night sessions to rearrange the presentation of issues.

But while the internal politicking raged, three issues attracted near unanimity. The miners agreed to a one-year assessment of 10 cents a week each (or about $800,000 total) to support the UMW's recently formed coal miners political action committee, which will lobby for their interests. With barely a second thought, they approved a host of expensive bargaining goals emphasizing tougher safety guarantees and fringe benefits. And they sent to the coal industry and the government a message reflecting their recent frustrations. Unless we get sizeable gains, it went, there's going to be a strike next Nov. 12 (when the current contract expires).

The delegates, mindful of the dictatorial control of past UMW leaders, balked at first at a constitutional article empowering the international to suspend or limit the autonomy of districts and locals for specified transgressions. But after a heated debate, the measure passed by a narrow majority, and it seemed that Mr. Miller had unified the convention. But in the final four days of the convention, that facade crumbled.

The first important stumbling block came on a vote to approve an administration-backed dues increase of $4 per active member, to $9.75 monthly. The money was to be split one-third each to a man's local, his district and the international. But the delegates wanted more money for their locals and districts and on the UMW's first roll call vote since 1936 they voted down the administration's proposal. An open forum then was held at which it was determined that the delegates wanted $4 at the regional levels. So both sides compromised, keeping the percentage split and raising the total to $12, a figure that passed easily.

Each side claimed victory, but most observers felt the administration had come up shorthanded on two important counts. The increased money the locals and districts won likely will give them more freedom than the international wants them to have, at least until Mr. Miller can more firmly consolidate his support. And miners from some districts deluged their delegates with complaints on the larger-than-expected dues increase. This, in turn, helped scotch an administration-backed $100 million strike fund proposal, which failed the next day.

The Bitterest Issue

Then came the bitterest issue of the whole convention—pensioner rights. The constitution committee proposed formally disbanding locals with fewer than 10 working members and transferring retirees in such "bogus" locals to nearby active groups. Mr. Miller's aim, he said, was to stop union corruption and the mistreatment and manipulation of elderly retirees by candidates for union office seeking their votes. But the issue became an emotional rallying point for the anti-Miller groups, whose loud protests sent the proposal back to committee.

On the next-to-last day of the convention, Mr. Miller's forces succeeded in reintroducing the "bogus locals" proposal, and getting it passed unchanged.

But this victory turned into a stunning defeat the following day on what was to have been the convention's crowning touch—approval of the streamlined grievance procedures. Mr. Miller already had negotiated with the coal operators and his staff thought the measure would be approved easily. But the ingrained coal miner's distrust of big business and his own union's leadership, combined with the thirst of Mr. Miller's opponents to retaliate for his actions the day before, was enough to stymie what the delegates saw as last-minute sleight of hand.

The defeat was ironic. Mr. Miller was not bound by either the union's constitution or the contract to submit the proposal to the delegates. And it was voted down largely by Boyle supporters though Mr. Boyle himself had initiated talks towards such a revision back in 1971.

Taken as a whole, the convention moved the UMW toward more open decision-making and more aggressive representation of its members. But the new rights bring with them difficult problems.

Not only is the convention's collective bargaining report shocking in the size of the goals it lists, it's also specific. For instance, it includes a demand that royalty coal operators payments into the union's welfare and retirement fund be tripled from 80 cents a ton on UMW-mined coal to $2.40 over the course of a three-year contract dating from the expiration of the current contract next Nov. 12. The extra money would be used to raise pensions to $500 a month from $150 now, as well as create dental and optical care programs and other fringe benefits.

The demands also call for a cost-of-living wage escalator of about one cent an hour for each 0.35 percentage point rise in the Labor Department's Consumer Price Index. And it demands 30 days a year of paid sick leave compared with none now—a goal the delegates listed first in their voting on bargaining priorities—as well as four weeks' vacation a year compared to two now.

Putting It on Paper

The trouble with publicizing such specific goals, one district president says, is that "when you put it on paper, a coal miner thinks he's going to get it." That, plus the failure of the revised grievance procedure, means that Mr. Miller's staff and the union's district officers have a formidable communication task to perform if rank and file contract ratification is to work.

Mr. Miller, in his first try, made a favorable impression on most of the delegates, much as he has with his industry counterparts. "He's honest, sincere ... pick any good adjective and it applies to him," comments the chief executive of a large coal company.

Nevertheless, there were times during the convention when the UMW chief failed to display the assertive leadership role he'll have to assume if he is to sell a less than perfect contract to his own district leaders, who must, in turn, sell it to the rank and file. By convention's end, even some pro-Miller delegates were complaining, "We've got too much democracy in our union."

UNIONS AND HEALTH CARE

By James C. Hyatt
Staff Reporter of The Wall Street Journal

WASHINGTON — Many of the nation's hospitals are facing an unprecedented surge of union organizing and pressure for higher pay.

Legislation approved by Congress this month and just signed by President Nixon removes from the National Labor Relations Act an exemption for nonprofit private hospitals. The change extends the law's protection to their employes.

So at least five AFL-CIO unions are making plans to sign up large numbers of the 1.5 million workers in the nation's more than 3,300 nonprofit private hospitals. Fewer than 300,000 of them currently belong to unions.

Where union organizers succeed, hospitals are certain to find their costs climbing even higher than now. Labor's bargainers will undoubtedly put pay rises first and foremost; wages for nonprofessional hospital employes are low by most standards. The Labor Department says average hourly earnings of hospital employes were $3.33 an hour in March, 73 cents an hour less than the average for manufacturing employes. "You can't run hospitals at the expense of the employes," one eager organizer insists. But the American Hospital Association is fearful of increased costs and strikes at hospitals where employes sign up with unions.

Congressional sponsors, led by Sen. Robert Taft Jr. of Ohio, insist that the just-passed measure will reduce the number of strikes in the health-care industry. They say fewer unions will have to strike to win employer recognition; such strikes are banned within the scope of the National Labor Relations Act. The sponsors add that the new law's mandatory mediation provisions will help discourage walkouts. They point to a recent three-week strike by 4,400 nurses against 42 hospitals in the San Francisco area; the dispute might have been prevented by mediation.

How the Act Works

Hospital workers are already free to form unions, but nonprofit private hospitals haven't been subject to the National Labor Relations Act and so haven't had to recognize unions. The exemption, a Senate committee found earlier this year, has "resulted in numerous instances of recognition strikes and picketing. Coverage under the act should completely eliminate the need for any such activity."

When covered by the act, a union will be able to request a representation election by presenting cards signed by 30% of the employes in a hospital; an election would be conducted by the National Labor Relations Board.

The major unions backing the legislation, however, made a number of concessions to help ensure that a hospital labor dispute won't interrupt patient care and to try to speed a settlement:

—A union couldn't strike or picket without giving 10 days' notice: the provision is designed to permit a hospital "to make arrangements for the continuity of patient care," the Senate committee said.

—A hospital or a union would have to give 90 days' notice before terminating or seeking to modify a collective bargaining contract, 30 days more than the act requires of other unions.

—A labor dispute in a health-care institution would be automatically subject to mediation by the Federal Mediation and Conciliation Service. The service could set up a fact-finding board to make recommendations for settlement; the board would be established 30 days before the contract expires and would report 15 days before expiration.

Still, the hospital association is unhappy with the legislation; officials had sought a provision requiring an additional 60-day "cooling-off" period. "If we had gotten that cooling-off period, you would have seen some reduction in strikes," an official says.

"To the extent you have more extensive collective bargaining," he adds, "you'll have increased costs. But that doesn't mean every hospital is going to be unionized." Nonetheless, union competition to organize hospitals will be intense.

"A Magna Carta"

The biggest push is planned by the Service Employees International Union, which already represents 200,000 health-care workers. The new law will be "a Magna Carta for over a million Americans," says George Hardy, president of the union. He asserts that it will "provide a way out of poverty for virtually the poorest-paid workers in the country." Some officials of this union talk of possibly doubling the size of the 500,000-member union in the next few years, mainly through hospital-organizing efforts.

"We have all kinds of units just waiting passage of the law," reports an official of the Laborers International Union. "In one town down in the South, we have about 9,000 authorization cards. That's going to be repeated in a number of other places."

The American Federation of State, County and Municipal Employes also plans a major organizing effort. "We're going to go at it very heavily," a spokesman says. The union currently has about 25,000 members in private nonprofit hospitals.

In addition, the Retail Clerks International Association has created a division to organize doctors, nurses, pharmacists, lab technicians, licensed practical nurses and other hospital personnel. The National Union of Hospital and Health Care Employes—an affiliate of the Retail, Wholesale and Department Store Union—will step up its organizing. And the Teamsters Union is expected to get busy among hospital workers.

Current Benefits

Unions currently representing hospital workers say their contracts have produced higher wages and benefits as well as chances for workers to advance to better jobs. "A lot of our locals have upgrading programs written into the contract," one union official says, "so with job experience and outside training, employes can work their way up." A nurse's aide, for example, might become a licensed practical nurse. "With few exceptions," he adds, "unorganized hospital workers get the minimum wage or within a dime of it," in contrast to higher union-negotiated rates.

Recently, Service Employes Local 880 in Boston negotiated its first contract with Jordan Hospital in Plymouth, Mass., resulting in an average wage increase of 18% over 15 months. A union official says the starting wage at the hospital moved up from $2 an hour to $2.41 four months after the contract took effect. The contract provided the first pay premium for night work, an extra 50 cents an hour for holiday work, and improved vacations—four weeks after 10 years instead of three weeks.

The coming union move into nonprofit hospitals is certain to bring a heap of cases before the National Labor Relations Board. Although the new legislation and congressional reports specifically suggest a number of interpretations to the board, "a great deal of litigation will probably be necessary" on certain points, predicts Peter G. Nash, the NLRB's general counsel.

For instance, he says, a union wouldn't have to give the 10-day strike notice in a case where an employer had committed an unfair labor practice. Similarly, he adds, the notice presumably wouldn't be valid if an employer used the 10-day warning to "undermine the bargaining relationship" by such actions as hiring large numbers of replacement workers or "receiving extraordinary amounts of supplies."

"Quite clearly," Mr. Nash observes, "Congress intended that a health-care institution was to have a 10-day period in which to plan its affairs so that the lives and health of its patients wouldn't be jeopardized by union economic action." At the same time, he suggests, the time couldn't be used to change "the relative economic strengths of the parties."

ORGANIZATION DRIVE

By TERRY P. BROWN
Staff Reporter of THE WALL STREET JOURNAL

They haven't yet taken to forming picket lines, but the nation's engineers are becoming increasingly, and often militantly, pro-union. Many of the men and women in the engineering community who until only recently scorned union affiliation as "nonprofessional" now are turning to organized labor for inspiration and assistance.

"The engineer now realizes he's vulnerable and expendable like everyone else," asserts Jack Golodner, director of the Council of AFL-CIO Unions for Scientific, Professional and Cultural Employes. "We're getting a good response to our organizing efforts."

The unionization movement among engineers has been under way for several years, but until recently it was on a limited scale. There are over one million engineers in the U.S., and about 5% belong to the two dozen independent professional unions that have for years engaged in collective bargaining at various companies. A few belong to affiliates of the major trade unions. But union men and engineers agree the 5% figure is expected to increase, probably dramatically, in the near future.

There is much activity already. New independent unions are being formed by engineers around the country. Major AFL-CIO affiliates are launching organization drives. Union-like political action groups are being established to press for resumption of funding on a major scale of government technical programs. And, perhaps most important, several of the old-line engineering technical societies, to which almost all engineers belong, are broadening their traditional educational and standard-setting roles and are setting up union-like economic programs for their members.

Cutbacks and Joblessness

The underlying reasons for all this activity are clear-cut. Cutbacks in government aerospace and defense budgets, coupled with a soft economy, have caused the highest unemployment in the engineering profession since the Depression. About 35,000 engineers are on the jobless rolls—more than three times the number in the early and middle 1960s. And it's estimated that as many as 65,000 more are working only part-time in their profession or have taken nonengineering jobs.

The salaries of employed engineers, to be sure, continue to be relatively high (the median salary for an engineer with 10 years of experience stands at more than $15,000). Nevertheless, the plight of their unemployed colleagues has had a profound psychological effect on even those with good engineering jobs. "Many of these guys got into engineering in the '50s and '60s because government and industry told them they'd always have secure and well-paying jobs," says Prof. Paul H. Thompson of Harvard Business School. "Now they are bitter and angry, and they feel they have been betrayed."

This sense of betrayal has been especially keen on the West Coast, with its large concentration of technical and research-oriented firms. Consequently, unions have made their greatest inroads among engineers in this area. Last November, for example, the Southern California Professional Engineering Association, an independent union representing more than 5,000 employes of McDonnell Douglas Corp. in California and Tulsa, missed affiliating with the Marine Engineers Beneficial Association

(AFL-CIO) by less than 1% of the members' vote (a majority vote was required).

Changing Times

"Even though the AFL-CIO lost, you can't ignore the fact that almost half of our members wanted to join a larger, more powerful labor organization," says Robert Leventhal, executive director of the Southern California group. "Five years ago, you couldn't find 5% of any engineering group that would favor joining organized labor."

Encouraged by growing unionist enthusiasm among engineers, the AFL-CIO has stepped up its recruiting efforts. The American Federation of Technical Engineers (AFL-CIO) is currently attempting to organize some 2,000 engineers and scientists at the Huntsville, Ala., facility of the National Aeronautics and Space Administration. The same group is also seeking recognition from San Francisco officials to represent the city's publicly employed professional engineers.

The United Auto Workers union at its April convention will consider by-law revisions that would allow professional organizations to retain their own name and much of their autonomy after UAW affiliation. In the meantime, the UAW has kicked off an organizing drive among professional engineers at several aerospace concerns in the Los Angeles area.

Many engineers, however, continue to remain wary of large labor organizations and fear being swallowed by groups that they consider too large, too impersonal and too unresponsive to individual initiative. Furthermore, they say, they dislike such hallmarks of traditional labor union contracts as job classifications and seniority. For these reasons, many engineers desiring representation of some sort have turned to independent unions.

A number of the independent unions have been formed in the construction and design industries, which employ large numbers of engineers. In San Francisco, for example, the three-year-old Organization of Architectural Employes last fall won the right to bargain for some 150 employes at three out of nine firms where elections were held. And in Detroit, the Architectural-Engineering Employes Union (less than a year old) is currently trying to organize some 5,000 engineers and architects and will soon call elections at several major firms.

"We're receiving advice from organized labor," says James J. Skalski, the Detroit group's chairman. "We'd like to stay independent, but if management doesn't develop a more enlightened attitude we might be forced to move" in the direction of big-time organized labor.

According to labor sources, nearly all engineers currently in collective bargaining units belong to independent unions; fewer than 1% of the nation's engineers are members of the large, traditional union groups. And despite the growing interest among engineers in organization, some still remain wary of affiliation with any bargaining group at all.

In an attempt to overcome this wariness, the California Society of Professional Engineers, a state chapter of the National Society of Professional Engineers, last June devised an alternative for engineers who want representation but who don't want to join a labor union. The alternative consisted of an "affiliation agreement" with the Western Council of Engineers, an Oakland-based independent union representing more than 700 publicly employed engineers.

The affiliation agreement, among other provisions, has opened discussion channels between the society, which under state law can't engage in collective bargaining, and the council, which can bargain collectively. According to Robert J. Kuntz, a member of the society's executive committee, the agreement means that "the professional society can provide a common meeting ground for both employe and employer, without the profession falling into the hands of organized labor."

Shedding Economic Indifference

The autonomous engineering societies, which number more than 150 and whose membership comprise most of the engineers in the U.S., have traditionally limited their activities to the publishing of technical journals and the establishment of ethical and educational standards. Until recently, the societies shunned involvement in nontechnical problems affecting their members for fear of losing their tax-exempt status as educational and scientific nonprofit organizations. But charges from members that the societies have tended to be management-oriented have caused several groups to shed their previous indifference toward economic issues.

As one case in point, the 66,000-member American Society of Civil Engineers prepared and distributed to employers a manual outlining certain principles of employment ranging from recruitment to working conditions. The society also plans to distribute specific salary guidelines later this year.

"We hope employers will voluntarily adopt these guidelines," says W. H. Wisely, the society's executive director. "We're not turning into a union, but we're taking a more realistic role—and maybe we can bring economic improvements through responsible leadership."

Other national technical societies are involved in pension-plan studies, job-assistance services and career-development programs. The 100,000-member American Chemical Society, for example, recently established an independent, nonprofit corporation that is attempting to set up a national pension system for professional engineers and scientists; the system would also be "portable," meaning that benefits would continue when an engineer moved from one job to another. (No such system currently exists, and many engineers have recently lost accrued benefits after being laid off or after they switched jobs.)

Skirting Limitations

In a different attempt to skirt their limitations, some societies have recently affiliated with the National Society of Professional Engineers, a nontechnical group that lobbies in Washington for legislation to aid its 65,000 full-time members. Last year, the Institute of Electrical and Electronics Engineers arranged for its members to join the National Society on either a full-time or associate basis (associate members can't vote). And other societies have since followed suit in order to give their members a say in nontechnical matters affecting the profession.

But some engineers want more from their societies. "A society must do more than set up study committees and then sit around and wring hands," asserts Irwin Feerst, a consulting electronics engineer from Massapequa Park, N.Y., and a member of the Institute of Electrical and Electronics Engineers. Mr. Feerst recently ran on a write-in campaign for the IEEE presidency on a platform primarily designed to make the society more active in protecting the economic status of its members. Although he was overwhelmingly defeated, he says he entered the election late and has subsequently gained increasing support. "I'm going to win next time, and the society will never be the same," he asserts.

Outside of societies, independent unions and large labor organizations, a number of engineers have formed ad hoc activist groups to lobby on their own for legislation providing employment for engineers and to support political candidates sympathetic to the technical community. While such groups are currently small and scattered, many of their members say their effectiveness is evidenced in an increasing number of congressional bills involving engineers and the White House's push for programs such as the proposed space shuttle.

A Powerful Voice

"Engineers have to overcome their parochialisms and work for a single powerful voice," says the spokesman for one group. "We'd like to see the National Society of Professional Engineers assume this role, but it presently only represents about 6% of the profession. In the meantime, we have to work to improve our national technical posture."

The ultimate effectiveness of such groups—and, indeed, of the entire organization effort among engineers—won't be known for some time to come and will be influenced to no small degree by external factors such as the number of graduating engineers arriving each year at the job front. An encouraging sign in this area is the fact that, according to estimates by the American Society for Engineering Education, national freshman engineering enrollments last fall dropped more than 16%. This statistic caused some observers to predict the current surplus of engineers may become a shortage by the end of the decade.

For the time being, however, the technical community feels the job outlook for engineers will remain bleak—a factor that should provide increasing impetus for nascent organization efforts. "It looks as though fields like housing, transportation and pollution-control aren't likely to take up the employment slack that's been created," says Prof. Eli Ginzberg, a Columbia University manpower expert. "We have a permanent softening in the demand for engineers that looks like it will last for several years."

HOSPITAL MILITANTS

By JOANN S. LUBLIN
Staff Reporter of THE WALL STREET JOURNAL

OAKLAND, Calif.—A strange labor dispute jammed nearly every bed at Highland General Hospital here last June. It was led by interns and residents who hospitalized many people who previously would have been turned away or treated as outpatients.

Soon beds began replacing tables in conference rooms. One night nurses were forced to put patients in a hallway. Meantime, the 110 interns and residents voluntarily stepped up their workweek—from a normal 80 hours to almost 120 hours during the 12-day protest—to care for the overflow patient load.

The house staff of interns and residents devised the protest, or "heal-in," to promote demands for better medical facilities and, not so incidentally, to obtain higher pay. Salaries, with no extra pay for overtime, worked out to $2.12 an hour for interns. (Laundry helpers at the hospital made $2.82.) Because the young staff doctors didn't want to strike, which would bring charges that they had abandoned their oath to heal the sick, they hit upon the heal-in tactic as a way to pressure hospital administrators.

"Morally Wrong"—but a 5% Pay Rise

And they won. The outraged director of the county-operated hospital called the protest "unethical" and "morally wrong." The county's labor negotiator threatened to call out the National Guard. But in the end the interns and residents won a 5% pay increase plus two weeks of extra vacation. And patients were promised expanded x-ray services, a night lab technician and a specialist trained in treating chest diseases.

The settlement was a victory for the Highland Association of Interns and Residents, or HAIR, a kind of combination trade union and professional club. The association is officially recognized as a collective-bargaining agent for the doctors by Alameda County, which includes Oakland.

As Highland's protest suggests, young doctors-in-training are growing restless. And an increasing number of them are turning to collective bargaining through house-staff associations to force better working conditions for themselves and higher-quality patient care.

A recent national survey found house-staff associations at 70% of all hospitals and at 81% of hospitals run by local and state governments. In the survey, conducted by The Hospital Physician, a trade publication, house-staff doctors said their associations scored greater successes in raising wages than in bettering hospital care.

"Below Poverty Levels"

That isn't surprising, The Hospital Physician said. "Stipends have been unrealistic in many areas, and they are below poverty-income levels in some," it asserted. As recently as 1966 the average intern earned $3,810 a year. By 1970 his annual paycheck had risen to $8,500, thanks partly to aggressive collective bargaining by house-staff associations on the East and West Coasts. But for an intern with a family to support and medical-school loans to repay, even $8,500 was often insufficient. His salary fell nearly $2,200 below the adequate standard of living for a family of four, as set by the U.S. Bureau of Labor Statistics. The House Physician said that the comparable figures for residents, who have already completed their internships, were $4,870 in 1966 and $9,600 in 1970.

The effect of increasing house staff salaries

on overall medical costs has been highly-disputed. Robert A. Derzon, director of hospitals and clinics for the University of California in San Francisco, estimates hospitals currently spend $500 million to maintain and train house staffs—less than 4% of the nation's annual $14.2 billion medical bill for physicians.

If hospitals replaced house staffs with full-fledged physicians from the community, medical costs would skyrocket further, interns and residents argue. So house staff costs, they say, are in fact a "savings."

About 55,000 recent medical-school graduates make up the house staffs of 1,500 U.S. hospitals. In many states a new graduate must serve a hospital internship before receiving a license for general practice. Further residency at a hospital under the tutelage of experienced specialists is required to obtain certification in a specialty such as surgery or obstetrics. In their two to seven years of internship and residency, house-staff members provide much of the day-to-day medical care in hospitals, especially major public hospitals in urban areas.

The Highland General house-staff association here is among the few officially recognized as collective-bargaining agents for doctors-in-training. As an affiliate of the Alameda County Employes Association, it is also perhaps the only one connected with a nonmedical union, according to Dr. Anthony Bottone, former house-staff president at the University of California Medical Center in San Francisco.

The Push for Recognition

House staffs in other places, such as New York, Chicago, Los Angeles, Philadelphia and Ann Arbor, have sought collective-bargaining recognition, from their hospitals or local governments or state labor-relations boards. Their efforts point up the increasing thrust of house-staff groups into labor organizing and bargaining. The trend was also evident at a Berkeley conference in January on collective bargaining and the young doctor, which drew three times the expected number of participants.

One conference speaker, Walter L. Kintz, an attorney for the National Labor Relations Board, says associations like HAIR represent "a new breed of socially responsible doctors wanting to change the structure of medicine." The doctors themselves agree. Dr. Gerald Smith, current HAIR president and a second-year resident in radiology, says the heal-in was a last-ditch effort to "show (administrators) who runs this hospital."

What happened at Highland General has its roots in organizing efforts elsewhere. A key pioneer was the Committee of Interns and Residents, or CIR, formed in New York in 1957.

New York's CIR has laid much of the groundwork for transforming house-staff associations into more militant and aggressive union-like groups. With a full-time staff, newspaper and dues checkoff, the CIR represents nearly 1,200 interns and residents (both physicians and dentists) at 18 municipal hospitals. The CIR also negotiates contracts for house-staff associations at seven voluntary (private) nonprofit hospitals.

The committee also wields substantial clout at city hall and in the state legislature, drafting health-care legislation, exposing poor hospital conditions to the media and protesting medical-budget cuts. "We know who to deal with. We have tremendous leverage," asserts Murray Gordon, the CIR's fast-talking, hard-driving attorney. Last spring an independent fact-finding panel resolved a contract stalemate between the CIR and the city's Health and Hospitals Corporation by providing pay increases averaging $2,500 over two years and a package of benefits.

Despite the CIR's successes, the unionizing path for house staffs seems strewn with more thorns than roses. At the recent Berkeley conference, one lawyer noted that only 22 states permit public employes to form unions. And just 12 states—including New York, Michigan and Pennsylvania—include voluntary nonprofit hospitals in their bargaining statutes.

Another thorn is traditional professional resistance to unionizing. That attitude has changed gradually as professionals in other fields—from college professors to social workers—have formed collective-bargaining units, says Dr. Bottone, who organized the Berkeley conference. Yet the most socially committed of interns and residents in HAIR still avoid the term "union" to describe their house-staff association. They shouldn't worry about terms, Mr. Gordon the CIR attorney, argues, "The fact that you have to use the term labor organization or even union is really a meaningless shibboleth because the organization is what you make of it," he says.

The Quality of Hospital Care

A multitude of more complex problems related to the house-staff organizing trend were debated at the Berkeley conference. Among the major issues discussed was whether the quality of a hospital's health care can be negotiated in a house-staff contract.

Part of the problem here, explains Mr. Kintz, the NLRB attorney, is that old-fashioned labor laws, designed for blue-collar factory settings, don't fit, "particularly where a professional has moral and legal responsibilities."

Under federal law, care of hospital patients would be viewed as the employer's product, not the house staff's working conditions. For interns and residents to include patient-care demands in their bargaining "is the same as bargaining about a 400-horsepower engine with auto workers," Mr. Kintz says.

Yet this issue helped ignite the recent house-staff unrest at Highland General. Dr. James C. Malcolm, director of the County Health Care Services Agency, would discuss but not "negotiate" on HAIR's demands for improved angiography and pulmonary physiology—that is, services concerning blood-vessel x rays and lung diseases.

"There are some things that are management prerogatives," the 57-year-old administrator asserts. "The ultimate decision on the quantity and quality of service here rests with the board of supervisors . . . and I'm their agent."

Dr. Len Saputo, last year's HAIR president, retorts that "I took the Hippocratic oath . . . and that oath tells me I don't give a damn what the administrator says" about patient care's being his prerogative.

Employes or Students?

Another key issue is whether interns and residents are employes or are students getting advanced training at hospitals. If they are students, some critics ask, why should they be paid a "living wage" or given employe benefits?

The whole question of the status of house-staff employes has stymied organizing efforts by staff associations in Ann Arbor and Philadelphia as courts and commissions spend months wrangling over the issue. In Ann Arbor, the University of Michigan Interns-Resident Association sought collective-bargaining recognition for its 550 members two years ago. Last March the Michigan Employment Relations Commission ruled that they were public employes with the right to organize. However, using the argument that house-staff members are trainees, the university appealed the commission's decision and won, in January, in the state court of appeals.

In Philadelphia in the fall of 1970, about 400 interns and residents from four hospitals sought to open a citywide house-staff organization modeled after the CIR. The hospital administrators' reaction to the prospect was "apoplectic," says Dr. James Sobel, president of the Philadelphia Association of Interns and Residents (PAIR). "They brought the whole thing up again that all you're interested in is money—and the argument that you're students." Dr. Sobel is a senior resident in medicine at the Albert Einstein Medical Center.

Last December the Pennsylvania Labor Relations Board ruled that house staffs are more students than workers and thus that "compensation . . . is the least important factor." Indeed, the board said, "personal sacrifice in order to complete their education . . . may even be necessary in order to condition them to more adequately and unselfishly serve the health needs of our citizens."

The "Payoff"

Another issue is whether house-staff associations can keep their hospitals from "buying off" members with large pay increases. Some of the more activist young physicians argue that house staffers become self-satisfied after big pay rises, squelching organizing efforts as well as attempts to push improvements in medical care.

This is what allegedly happened at Los Angeles County Hospital, where only a minority of the house-staff association supported a heal-in two years ago. About 100 residents in internal medicine organized the action to protest alleged overcrowding and inadequate medical treatment in the 2,000-bed hospital complex, according to Dr. Rex Greene, association president and a second-year resident in internal medicine.

But the heal-in ended after a few weeks when most of the 750-member association voted to accept a 35% pay rise. The increase and subsequent cost-of-living rises put Los Angeles County Hospital in one of the country's highest wage brackets for house staffs. Consequently, most house-staff doctors at the hospital "are very nouveau riche and so they seduce themselves out of worrying about hospital conditions," Dr. Greene says bitterly.

To many hospital officials, the newly militant interns and residents pose a threat to health care because their associations someday may resort to slowdowns or strikes. "A union is a union, whether professional or not," says Grover Clark, personnel director for Beth Israel Medical Center in New York. "If there is a strike, some patient dies someplace."

The young doctors deny that they would even consider use of the strike. "Walking off the job is irresponsible," says Dr. Mickey Ruxin, a Highland General intern. Dr. Smith, the president of HAIR, agrees, adding that if other county workers at the hospital strike, "the last way (for doctors) to support them is to go on strike."

ROCKING THE BOAT

By Neil Maxwell
Staff Reporter of The Wall Street Journal

JOHNSONVILLE, S.C.—This sleepy Southern town took school integration in its stride. It scarcely winced when the tiny local library stocked "Portnoy's Complaint." But to hear town elders tell it, Johnsonville now faces a *real* menace: unions.

Last year, the Textile Workers Union of America sent a pair of organizers—one white, one black—to unionize Wellman Industries Inc., a textile producer that is by far the area's largest employer. The battle that has split this town ever since throws light on the state of union organizing that still exists in much of rural Dixie. It's a far cry from conditions that businessmen face in Northern cities.

When union organizers distribute leaflets to workers, police cars suddenly park nearby. A worker claims he was fired for wearing a union sticker on his shirt. The bulletin of the First Baptist Church in nearby Hemingway prints invitations to anti-union rallies. And the local school system at one point distributed anti-union notices in classrooms for children to take home.

Lagging Wages

The whole town is involved because the whole town thinks its future may be at stake. Nonsense, reply union men. Without unionization, this town of 900 will always be a low-income place, the union men say. They claim Wellman wages, ranging from $1.73 to $2.49 an hour, average $2.20 an hour. (The company says the average is around $2.40.) In any event, this average is considerably below national factory pay and even below the $2.55 to $2.79 hourly wages that unionized textile plants in the state pay, union men say.

But with growing competition from cheap foreign textiles, Wellman says it can't boost wages dramatically. Indeed, rising costs and tougher foreign competition are bankrupting many textile plants and thus stranding textile towns like this one.

Business leaders note that it was largely low labor costs that attracted Wellman here from the highly unionized Boston area back in 1954. Could the company move again? "I was afraid Wellman would go to Mexico or Europe or someplace and leave Johnsonville dead like it was before they came here," says Jim McCall, operator of a heating and air conditioning business here and a former union man himself.

At Wellman itself, the race has been neck and neck. In the first representation election, Wellman workers last October voted against unionization—but by 420 votes to 398. The fight may reach a climax soon. Today the National Labor Relations Board will hold hearings to determine whether six Wellman workers were fired illegally for favoring the union. The union hopes the board not only will reinstate the workers with back pay but also will order a new election.

"Go-Go-Go TWUA"

In one of the cases, the company says it fired Jerry Bruce for posting pro-union stickers in the canteen area, a clear violation of rules. But all that is a misunderstanding, says Mr. Bruce. "All I was doing was wearing a 'Go-Go-Go TWUA' sticker on the back of my shirt," he says. He claims the company also wronged him by taking him off his regular job of wool finisher. "They put me to cleaning floors," he says. "I figure they were trying to dishearten me. I never saw a white boy doing that job—except me."

Even if the NLRB doesn't order a new election immediately, another is expected next October. In any event, the union plans a meeting next Sunday to launch a revitalized organizing drive.

Meanwhile, the alleged harassment continues. Indeed, union men say there has been one "misunderstanding" after another ever since the two organizers arrived and checked into the Coachman Inn, the only motel in Hemingway. The organizers say that as soon as the motel management found out who they were, they were told to vacate.

But that's a misunderstanding, says Merritt Morris, largest stockholder in the motel and undertaker for Hemingway's whites. (Blacks and whites here go to school together, but still get buried separately.) "We knew who they were when they registered; we even gave them a commercial rate," says Mr. Morris in the hushed parlor of his funeral home. He claims the white organizer left of his own accord after 10 weeks and the black one was asked to leave after six weeks because he repeatedly violated rules, such as the one against making telephone calls after 11 p.m.

Then the organizers bought a trailer and parked it just outside Hemingway. But the city refused to let them hook up to the water system. The organizers hooked up anyway. Then the city unhooked the pipe. The organizers promptly hooked up again. Finally the city hauled the water meter and the pipe away.

So the organizers filed a $100,000 suit against the mayor and five councilmen, charging harassment. But city officials say there's no harassment at all. It's just that the city has a water shortage, the trailer was outside city limits, and no new connections are being permitted in such cases, they claim. So the city filed charges against the organizers for violating a state law against hooking onto a water system illegally.

Then the owner of the land that the organizers rented to park their trailer soured on his tenants. "I'm a union man myself," he says. "But I never heard of union organizers doing any good by going into a place and stirring up trouble." So the owner ordered the organizers off the land immediately. The organizers refused to leave right away. So the angry owner built a fence around three sides of the trailer. Thus the only access to the trailer involved walking through a ditch. (The organizers moved to another town.)

Some local businessmen have fought the union nearly as enthusiastically as has Wellman itself. Mr. McCall, the heating man, and Mr. Morris, the undertaker, sponsored an anti-union rally in the school gymnasium. (Mr. Morris was on the school board at the time, but he claims the gym is available for any group.) Over 200 citizens attending the meeting heard a number of speeches vigorously denouncing the union and watched a film called "And Women Must Weep." The movie depicted union strike violence in Henderson, N.C., another textile town.

The union-management fight itself has also been acrimonious. Just in case Wellman workers were thinking of a strike, the company made its position clear: "All those who went out could be permanently replaced at the end of the strike. They would have no job and would not be entitled to any lost wages."

Since the organizing drive started, the company has erected powerful searchlights outside the plant. Union backers claim the lights are there largely to help identify workers who accept union literature as they drive in for the night shift.

Union men also claim it is a clear attempt at intimidation when police cars show up during a distribution of union literature.

Gary Cooper, the Johnsonville police chief, says that is all a misunderstanding. He concedes the plant is outside his police jurisdiction, but he says: "We were more or less just spectators. I pay highway taxes just like anybody else, so I got as much right out there as anybody else." Observers say it is only natural for the chief to take an interest in happenings at the plant, as his boss, the mayor, is on the plant security force.

The searchlights and police cars contribute to the high-security atmosphere at the plant. A high chain link fence topped with barbed wire surrounds the premises, and big gates block the entrances. As a visitor drives up to the guardhouse, a uniformed security agent puts down his copy of "Passion for a Price" to check the stranger's credentials. Only when the outsider is identified and his destination determined does the guard press a button to raise the gate.

Wellman executives also keep themselves generally closed off from the press. One of the few things they will tell a reporter is that they think reporters have given the company a bad press. They particularly dislike "Listening to America," a new book by Bill Moyers that has a chapter on Johnsonville.

Despite all this, many here consider John Wellman, the company president, an excellent employer and citizen. Paradoxically, the heavily guarded plant is a beautifully landscaped modern structure. Working conditions are better than in many Southern plants. The company has recently appointed two black supervisors. This may not sound like much, but it is a change in a town that still has service station restroom doors marked "white" and "colored."

Mr. Wellman enthusiastically boosts—and contributes to—various causes to improve the area. He sold land at a cheap price for a low-income housing project. When told that many of the new residents came from the tobacco and soybean farms in the area and were used to large vegetable gardens, he donated a half-acre of land for each tenant.

But union supporters charge "paternalism." And they point out that some Wellman workers earn so little, even working full-time, that they qualify for federal rent supplements.

UNIONS AND POLITICS

By Byron E. Calame
Staff Reporter of The Wall Street Journal

LOS ANGELES — Like the President himself, some of Richard Nixon's foes in organized labor have been surrendering sensitive political records.

The International Association of Machinists, in a case initiated by a group of dissident members of the union, was forced by a federal court here to release thousands of documents. They reveal in unusual detail how the IAM goes about electing its friends to federal office.

This rare glimpse into the inner workings of one of the AFL-CIO's largest (800,000 members) and most politically active unions shows that there is a lot more to a union's political clout than the direct financial contributions reported to government watchdogs—and labor's political experts say the machinists probably adhere to the campaign spending laws as closely as any union.

The documents indicate that direct gifts are often overshadowed by various services provided free of charge to favored candidates under the guise of "political education" for union members. The indirect aid includes some of labor's most potent political weapons; assignment of paid staff members to candidates' campaigns, use of union computers, mobilization of get-out-the-vote drives.

Trips and Dinners

Dues have also been used, the documents indicate, to supply IAM-backed candidates with polls and printing services and to finance "non-partisan" registration drives, trips by congressional incumbents back home during campaigns, and dinners benefiting office seekers endorsed by the machinists. Machinist-backed candidates are almost invariably Democrats.

An important question is whether these dues-financed activities violate federal laws that for decades have barred unions and corporations from using their treasury funds to contribute "anything of value" to candidates for federal office. Money for such direct contributions by unions must come from voluntary donations coaxed out of the members. The federal statutes do permit unions to spend dues for partisan politicking directed at the union's members and their families, on the theory that this sort of thing is internal union business, and the money used for this activity is called "education money," or "soft money."

The political activities of the machinists' union are, indeed, aimed at the union's members and are therefore proper, says William Holayter, director of the union's political arm, the Machinists Non-Partisan Political League.

Drawing the Line

Even labor's critics concede that it is sometimes hard to draw the line between activities designed to sell a candidate to a union's members and those intended to sway voters in general. A member of the machinists assigned to promote a candidate among other machinists may inevitably find himself wooing other voters as well.

Still, the machinists' documents suggest that the union has often sought to provide maximum assistance to a candidate by use of soft money. "The problem," says one labor political strategist, "is that the machinists put too much in writing." The late Don Ellinger, the widely respected head of the Machinists Non-Partisan Political League who died in 1972, evidently had a penchant for memos.

Spending reports filed with the Senate for

the 1970 campaign show that the Machinists Non-Partisan Political League openly gave Sen. Gale McGee $5,000; the internal records now disclose that the Wyoming Democrat also received at least $9,300 in noncash assistance. Direct donations to Texas Democrat Ralph Yarborough's unsuccessful Senate reelection bid in 1970 were listed at $8,950; one document indicates he got other help worth at least $10,680. While the league poured $15,200 directly into Democrat John Gilligan's unsuccessful 1968 bid for an Ohio Senate seat, the documents show it indirectly provided more, $15,500.

Receipt Unreported

Available records indicate that few, if any, campaign committees for machinist-backed candidates listed indirect aid from dues money as contributions. Prior to a 1972 toughening of disclosure requirements, candidates evidently found it easy to spot loopholes that were used to avoid reporting such indirect assistance.

The dissident machinists who forced disclosure of their union's files had brought their suit with the backing of the National Right to Work Legal Defense Foundation. The dissidents wanted the court to bar the union from using dues money for any political activity—including such clearly legal endeavors as politicking directed at its own members and traditional union lobbying efforts. The real goal of the right-to-work foundation is to eliminate the forced payment of dues. A federal judge dismissed the suit Dec. 19, largely because the union offered to start rebating the dues of any member who disagrees with the union's stand on political or legislative issues. The dissident group appealed the decision Jan. 10.

One questionable arrangement of the machinists helped reelect Sen. McGee in 1970. Alexander Barkan, director of the AFL-CIO Committee on Political Education, asked the machinists early that year to put the names of 65,000 "Democrats in Wyoming" on the machinists' computer for the Senator's use in "mailings, registration, etc." The minutes of the Machinists Non-Partisan Political League executive committee show that Mr. Ellinger recommended handling the chore but warned that it would have to be financed with "general-fund money" (the league's separate kitty composed of voluntary donations) and would be considered "a contribution toward the Gale McGee campaign."

Despite the warning, internal records show that bills totaling $9,302.74 for the operation were paid out of the league's political-education fund, built from dues money. Computing & Software Inc. was paid $4,696.84, Minnesota Mining & Manufacturing Co. received $414, and $4,191.90 wen to reimburse the IAM treasury for cards it provided.

Doubts about such arrangements may be raised in the coming report by the Senate Watergate committee. Though Republican hopes for public hearings on union campaign contributions will probably be disappointed, the committee staff has asked unions broad and potentially explosive questions about the services provided to candidates.

Watergate revelations, some union politicians believe, have demonstrated that labor can never collect enough rank-and-file donations to rival campaign contributions by business bigwigs. "There is no way we can match them," says Mr. Holayter of the machinists. "It's silly to try." Hence the importance of the indirect contributions.

This is one reason why the AFL-CIO is pressing for public financing of federal campaigns; its strategists obviously figure that a ban on direct contributions would leave labor in a better position relative to business than it is in now.

Past Performance

If past performance is any guide, the machinists' union would still be a valuable supporter for its political favorites if public financing were adopted. Its indirect assistance in staffers' time alone has totaled in the tens of thousands of dollars, the court documents show.

Printing is another campaign expense that the IAM often helps its friends meet. With the 1970 elections coming up, an aide to Rep. Lloyd Meeds passed to the machinists a bill for the printing of the Washington Democrat's quarterly newsletter. "The newsletter went to every home in the Second District," the aide rejoiced in one of the released documents. "We had a tremendous, positive response to it." Although the newsletter had been distributed far beyond the IAM's ranks in an election year, a soft-money check for $695.17 to the printer was quickly dispatched to a local union official.

Early in the 1972 reelection drive of Sen. Thomas McIntyre, the Machinists Non-Partisan Political League agreed to spend $1,000 "for assistance in newsletters" put out by the New Hampshire Democrat. And earlier, during Rep. John Tunney's successful 1970 bid for a California Senate seat, the league picked up a $1,740 tab for printing of a brochure that compared the Democrat's voting record with that of the GOP incumbent, George Murphy. Some of the brochures were passed out at a county fair.

The amount of union staff time devoted to candidates' campaigns is difficult to pin down. Irving Ross, a certified public accountant retained by the suing dissident machinists to analyze the IAM documents, filed an affidavit giving "incomplete" tabulations. Mr. Ross says the time that IAM "grand lodge representatives" and "special representatives" spent on campaigns in 1972 was worth $39,175. The amounts were $58,241 in 1970 and $42,921 in 1968, he says. The IAM says the figures are too high, but it didn't challenge them in court.

A status report prepared by the machinists political unit in late August 1970 shows that at least one field representative was working full time on each of over 20 congressional campaigns. IAM agents often become almost part of the candidate's campaign staff. When Robert Brown was assigned full time to Indiana Sen. Vance Hartke's reelection campaign in May 1970, he set up an office right in the Democrat's headquarters and had the title of chairman of the Indiana Labor Committee for Hartke. Another IAM representative, William Wolfe, was assigned to Yarborough campaigns in Texas in 1970 and 1972—and was being paid out of the union treasury in May 1972 even though a new law effective in April 1972 specifically barred a union from using dues money to pay for services rendered to a candidate, thus spelling out more clearly an old prohibition.

The union also takes machinists out of the shop for campaign duty, giving them "lost time" compensation out of dues money to make up for the loss of regular pay. Thus, the files show, two Baltimore machinists got $282.40 a week while working for the Humphrey presidential campaign for five weeks in 1968. A Maryland IAM official said later that the two "did a first-rate job, especially in smoking out the local Democratic politicians who were inclined to cut the top of the ticket" and persuading them not to do so.

I'm Free, Fly Me

Rep. Richard Hanna of California got $500 from the machinists to help finance a $6,000 "nonpartisan" registration effort to help get him reelected in 1970. In a letter requesting the union's aid, the Democrat predicted that the drive would "raise the district to at least 53.5% Democratic . . . because most of the unregistered voters are Democrats." He said the registrars would be preceded by "bird dogs," meaning that Democratic workers would roam out ahead of the registrar to identify residents of unregistered Hanna supporters.

The machinists' union's airline credit cards come in handy when incumbents are eager to get home in election years. Early in 1969, the executive committee of the machinist political unit authorized the expenditure of $3,600 to buy plane tickets home for unnamed "western Senators" during the following year's campaign. The league's "education fund" provided Sen. Yarborough and his aides with $705.30 worth of tickets during his 1970 reelection campaign. The files show that $500 went to Sen. Albert Gore, Democrat of Tennessee, during his losing reelecton effort in 1970.

Machinist officials contend the organization pays for such travel because the candidate speaks to a union group or "consults with union leadership" in his district. But correspondence in the files indicates that this is more of a rationalization than a reason. Take a 1969 Ellinger memo to Sen. Yarborough outlining procedures "for all transportation matters." It states:

"We would like our files to contain a letter . . . indicating that you intend to be in Texas on a particular date to consult with the leadership of our union. If a trip includes a member of your staff, the letter should also name the staff member as being included in the consultation."

"Appreciation dinners" for Senators and Representatives often serve as a conduit for "soft money." Consider the ten $100 tickets the IAM bought to a 1969 testimonial gathering for Sen. Frank Moss, Democrat of Utah, who faced an election in 1970. "Since Moss is not yet an announced candidate, we can use educational money for this event and later consider this as part of our overall contribution," the minutes of the league's executive committee explain.

UAW: 'CAUSES' vs. BREAD AND BUTTER

By Norman Pearlstine

Under Walter Reuther the United Auto Workers had a unique position in the American labor movement. The fiery redhead was a dreamer, a visionary. It was never enough for him that a union merely bargain for the bread-and-butter issues that affected his members. He constantly struggled for the causes he felt would help all people, and he surrounded himself with a cadre of social activists who shared his views.

None of these "little Reuthers" showed more promise of carrying on this tradition than did Paul Schrade. First as one of Mr. Reuther's assistants, and then as the union's West Coast regional director, the bearded, Yale-educated Mr. Schrade was said by many to possess the idealism that Mr. Reuther was constantly looking for in the younger officials who would one day run his union.

A. H. Raskin, The New York Times' labor expert, enthused in 1963 that Mr. Schrade, then 37 years old, was "the prototype of the labor leader of the future." The nation's intellectual establishment embraced him as one of its own, applauding his active support in innumerable social causes and his strong and early opposition to the Vietnam war. And he gained a national reputation as a liberal political figure when he was critically wounded by Sirhan Sirhan in the fusillade that killed Robert Kennedy, one of his closest friends.

Mr. Woodcock's Position

But Walter Reuther died in 1970, and many people think the UAW hasn't been pushing as hard on social issues since. Leonard Woodcock, who now runs the union, intellectually shares Mr. Reuther's idealism. But since coming to power, he has spent most of his time and energy dealing with the union's internal problems.

There has been no purge of the social activists who held positions throughout the UAW under Mr. Reuther. But many of them, including Mr. Reuther's brother, Victor, who played an active role in the union, have left it since Mr. Woodcock became its president. Unionists who worry primarily about wages and benefits and pay little attention to social issues seem to be gaining strength, and in many ways the UAW is becoming more and more like any other big union.

As a result, Mr. Schrade now finds himself in the middle of an uphill campaign for re-election as a regional director. His opponents, who now have a majority of the region's delegates behind them, have criticized Mr. Schrade for spending too much time on social problems and not enough attending to the union's day-to-day affairs.

Mr. Schrade withstood a similar challenge two years ago, but that was when Mr. Reuther was still alive to help him. This year he is much more on his own, and the election, which takes place tomorrow at the union's international convention in Atlantic City, may determine if there is still room for him and activists of his ilk in the UAW.

Mr. Reuther and Mr. Schrade didn't always agree. They split badly, for example, over the Vietnam war, which Mr. Reuther supported through most of the 1960s. Still, in the last two years Mr. Schrade has been one of the leading spiritual preservers of Mr. Reuther's idealism.

The West Coast director has been an active supporter and close adviser to Cesar

Chavez and the National Farm Workers Union. And he has been one of the guiding forces behind the Watts Labor Community Action Council and the East Los Angeles Community Union, two "community unions" that have worked for better schooling, housing and city services throughout the Los Angeles slums.

Mr. Schrade's Los Angeles headquarters, bedecked with posters and buttons supporting myriad causes, has at times looked more like a student center on a radical college campus than a union office. And at one time or another he has lent office space and other facilities to the farm workers, conservationists, a prisoners' union, a group trying to register students to vote, numerous antiwar organizations (Mr. Schrade himself has been a leading spokesman for the National "Set the Date" Committee), and many other groups of social activists.

None of this has sat very well with Mr. Woodcock, who has slowly pulled the UAW away from much of its commitment to social activism. The union under Mr. Woodcock has taken an active role in promoting a national health insurance program and no-fault auto insurance. And it continues to put out press releases that generally take a liberal position on many issues. But many of the projects that were important to Mr. Reuther have been abandoned or sharply curtailed.

The Alliance for Labor Action, a social action organization that Mr. Reuther and the Teamsters established in Washington to support union organizing, civil rights efforts and a host of other causes, is being dissolved. Neither union is contributing any money to the ALA, and the staff, which once included 50 persons, has been cut to one man, who will go as soon as the organization's furniture is sold.

And in Detroit, the UAW has all but given up on Mr. Reuther's efforts to promote improved housing in the city's slums. Contributions to the farm workers, another Reuther pet, have been severely cut back at the international union level. And support for development of "community unions" has nearly been abandoned.

Some of Mr. Woodcock's supporters insist that there has been no lag in the UAW's interest in social issues since he became the union's president and argue that the cutbacks in social programs were necessary only because the union is virtually broke and doesn't have the funds to continue them. But other insiders at Solidarity House, the union's headquarters in Detroit, say privately that since Mr. Woodcock came into power many good

social programs have been unable to get UAW support even though they would cost nothing to endorse.

Not surprisingly, Mr. Woodcock and Mr. Schrade show little affection for each other. Mr. Schrade says that Mr. Woodcock tried to get him defeated two years ago. In the days following Mr. Reuther's death, Mr. Schrade worked hard for Douglas Fraser, a UAW vice president who was campaigning against Mr. Woodcock to succeed Mr. Reuther. Mr. Woodcock has since criticized Mr. Schrade for the zealous way he supported Mr. Fraser.

At a meeting of aerospace workers on the West Coast a few months ago, Mr. Woodcock spoke warmly of Henry Lacayo, one of Mr. Schrade's chief opponents, and made no mention of the West Coast director. At a recent closed session of the UAW's international board, the union president delivered a lengthy criticism of Mr. Schrade in front of the other board members. It was only after UAW Secretary-Treasurer Emil Mazey, a founder of the union and one of its most articulate members, took control of the meeting that a resolution was passed endorsing Mr. Schrade's re-election as a director.

Mr. Schrade's Problems

Not that Mr. Schrade can blame all of his problems on Mr. Woodcock and the change in the union's direction. One reason Mr. Reuther could spend time on social issues was that he had a very competent staff of administrators who carried out much of the day-to-day job of running the union. Mr. Schrade concedes that some of his staff members haven't been as efficient as they could be in handling grievances and other problems involving union members.

In addition, Mr. Schrade hasn't spent as much time as a union director must ingratiating himself with the second level of union leaders, who control the votes that he needs to be re-elected. Some local presidents in his region complain that they rarely see him and that he never seeks their advice.

"The only time I ever see Paul Schrade is on a television talk show, advocating peace or the farm workers," complains one West Coast union official. "If he's not protesting with Joan Baez or Melina Mercouri, he's off in Washington playing politics with Teddy Kennedy," he adds.

Mr. Schrade says that he spends 98% of his time on union-related activities, but it doesn't seem that way to many of his members. And much of the time he does spend isn't on union activities that are fully appreciated by the man on the assembly line. For example, he organized a three-day seminar on the problem of imported cars and exported jobs, which was praised by those few members who attended it, but was generally ignored by many members and union officials.

On balance it appears that Mr. Schrade has made some important contributions to the UAW. Mr. Reuther once said that "a labor movement can get soft and flabby spiritually. It can make progress materially, and the soul of the union can die in the process."

The soul that concerned Mr. Reuther won't die if Mr. Schrade is defeated; other strong figures will work to keep its social activism alive. But a strong voice in support of that soul will be missing, and the UAW may not be the same without it.

LABOR'S DURABLE KING OF THE HILL

By BYRON E. CALAME

BAL HARBOUR, Fla. — George Meany's gavel is firmly controlling the flow of rhetoric and resolutions at the AFL-CIO's tenth biennial convention here.

The 79-year-old AFL-CIO president's tight rein on the convention symbolizes the influence he quietly wields day-to-day inside the 13.5-million member Federation. And his power to shape Federation policies depends on far more than a gavel or his title.

Casual observers sometimes assume the AFL-CIO is a monolithic institution automatically subservient to the tough-talking Mr. Meany. In fact, the AFL-CIO's union affiliates can walk out of the Federation anytime they get mad enough at Mr. Meany —as the United Auto Workers did in 1968 under the leadership of the fiery Walter Reuther.

Yet rebellions against Mr. Meany's rule seldom have occurred during the AFL-CIO's 20-year history—although Mr. Meany doesn't hesitate to impose his will even in some explosive situations. Just last year, for example, he kept the Federation neutral in the presidential campaign, despite the protests of several other labor leaders who wanted to back Democrat George McGovern against labor's old nemesis, Richard Nixon.

There's no single factor that enables Mr. Meany to shape an AFL-CIO consensus on many issues. Rather, his influence flows from shrewd manipulation of a complex array of factors, including some that might seem like mundane organizational matters.

Control over the Federation's lobbying priorities on Capitol Hill is a key source of Mr. Meany's strength. Thus, making a boost in the federal minimum wage the AFL-CIO's current prime legislative goal earns him the gratitude of labor leaders in the garment and service industries where a higher pay floor can spur increased union scales.

Making the minimum-wage issue a top objective isn't the uncontroversial decision it might seem. Leaders of the high-paid building trades, for example, would prefer more AFL-CIO emphasis on pushing a bill that would broaden their right to picket construction sites. But Mr. Meany can point to past favors for the building trades. For example, he directed AFL-CIO lobbyists to successfully push for a rule included in the general revenue-sharing law insuring that building tradesmen are paid prevailing union wages in construction projects financed by federal revenue-sharing funds.

Day-to-day lobbying tactics are equally important. Mr. Meany can please Jerry Wurf, president of the State, County and Municipal Employes Union, by instructing the AFL-CIO's team of lobbyists to hold out for coverage of public workers in any new minimum-wage bill. In the current give-and-take of hammering out a bill revamping the nation's private pension system, Mr. Meany can do favors for some unions by insisting a particular provision be kept in the legislation at all costs.

Mr. Meany's Recommendations

As the top spokesman for organized labor in Washington, Mr. Meany is consulted by both Democratic and Republican administrations on government appointments involving labor His say in appointments to government commissions, official delegations going abroad and even lower-level bureaucratic jobs means ambitious unionists have plenty to gain from Meany job recommendations.

Consider Paul Hall, the president of the Seafarers Union, who was indicted in 1970 in connection with alleged illegal political contributions. Some union men figured Mr. Hall's future had been dimmed by the charges although they were eventually dismissed. But Mr. Meany has stepped in to help polish up Mr. Hall's image. At the behest of the AFL-CIO president, Mr. Hall was named by President Nixon last year to both the new Industrial Peace Commission and the labor-management advisory committee to the Cost of Living Council. The grateful Mr. Hall toured the country last fall staunchly defending Mr. Meany's decision to remain neutral in the presidential campaign.

Mr. Meany can punish, too. Joseph Beirne, the pro-McGovern head of the Communications Workers of America who differed sharply with Mr. Meany's call for neutrality in the Nixon-McGovern campaign, had loyally followed the Federation president off the Productivity Commission when the AFL-CIO quit the Pay Board in March 1972. One result of their disagreement: Mr. Beirne wasn't renamed to the productivity panel when the AFL-CIO chief decided to rejoin it earlier this year.

The Federation chief also can bestow helpful publicity on union presidents. Mr. Meany has a lot to say about how a union leader or his organization are portrayed in the AFL-CIO's widely distributed newspaper and magazine. An example: A recent Labor Day address by Edward J. Carlough, the young president of the Sheetmetal Workers Union, caught Mr. Meany's fancy. A week or so later, lengthy excerpts from the speech appeared in the AFL-CIO News, giving Mr. Carlough some valuable exposure.

The degree of support the Federation gives an affiliate's boycott or strike is another lever of power for Mr. Meany. The Amalgamated Clothing Workers Union obviously is grateful for the wide attention its boycott of slacks made by El Paso-based Farah Manufacturing Co. has received in AFL-CIO publications. When local officials of other unions have read about the boycott in the AFL-CIO news, it makes it easier to get them to mobilize an anti-Farah drive in their city, an Amalgamated Clothing Workers official explains.

Financial dispensations for hard-pressed affiliates have been heavily influenced by Mr. Meany, although he can't unilaterally dispense such favors. Not long ago, for instance, the cash-short International Union of Electrical Workers got permission to suspend payments of its monthly head-tax to the Federation. And some affiliates are allowed to pay the AFL-CIO head-tax on fewer members than they publicly claim.

Harder to pinpoint, but extremely important, are Mr. Meany's strong personality and vast knowledge of the AFL-CIO and the people in it, based on his tenure as the only president of the Federation and as the head of the old American Federation of Labor before it merged with the Congress of Industrial Organizations.

His reservoir of experience often enables him to settle inter-union disputes speedily. Thus, two years ago, he quickly settled a dispute between Building Trades leaders and the United Steelworkers over representation of a particular group of construction workers. The Building Tradesmen protested when the USW proposed to take over representation of some construction workers as part of its merger with an independent union. But the Building Trades leaders rapidly abandoned their jurisdictional argument when Mr. Meany cited an historical precedent, going back to the old AFL days, for these particular construction workers to be represented by an industrial union like the USW rather than a Building Trades union.

The strongwilled Mr. Meany doesn't hesitate to use his position to shape broad policy even before it's debated in the Federation's policy-making Executive Council. He can effectively lock the Executive Council into a position, even before it meets, through the press coverage he can command as the AFL-CIO leader.

One example was the immediate support the hawkish Mr. Meany expressed for President Nixon's controversial decision to invade Cambodia in the spring of 1970. When the regular AFL-CIO Council meeting rolled around, the 33 union presidents who are members had little real choice: They could adopt a resolution generally in line with their leader's position—or repudiate him by issuing a weaker statement or none at all. The Council backed Mr. Meany.

Undercutting Sen. McGovern

Or consider how Mr. Meany undercut Sen. McGovern's Democratic candidacy last year. The AFL-CIO head authorized release of a "white paper" attacking the presidential nominee early in the Democratic Convention; the document had been prepared without consulting most Executive Council members. With Mr. Meany's anti-McGovern position laid out, a Council majority voted the following week to support the Meany call for neutrality. Yet about half the Council members went on to support McGovern themselves—struggling all the while to combat the impact of the AFL-CIO "white paper" the Nixon forces distributed widely.

The crafty Mr. Meany, however, seldom risks a fight unless he is certain of prevailing. He usually checks out carefully the sentiment among key union presidents and trusted advisers. Even some of his critics concede he has an uncanny knack for sensing the way the political winds are blowing. Thus, they admit that Mr. Meany accurately detected the distaste among many rank-and-filers for George McGovern's liberal positions on amnesty, welfare and abortion.

So when Mr. Meany speaks, most union leaders figure it's a good idea to listen. So do others—even in the Nixon administration. "It's really easier to find out where labor stands than to find out where business stands," says one Nixonite. "There's no one place you can touch base to find out where business stands. But with labor you just go check with Meany."

This administration attitude helps create a kind of chicken-and-egg situation. The fact that administration officials tend to consult with Mr. Meany further enhances his influence inside the Federation. And the AFL-CIO leader, despite the potshots he is taking at the White House during the Federation's convention, carefully keeps open at least one line of communication with the administration. In the current situation, it's Treasury Secretary George Shultz.

Thus, the often bold Mr. Meany seems to demonstrate that power begets power. Or, as one Meany biographer has concluded, the AFL-CIO president believes "power unused is power wasted." If that is indeed true, it's clear the canny AFL-CIO chief isn't a wastrel.

LABOR'S FUTURE

By Byron E. Calame
Staff Reporter of The Wall Street Journal

Crusty old George Meany, sojourning in the Florida sun after a bout of illness, is getting set to renew his domination of the labor movement.

Almost heedless of his 77 years, the AFL-CIO chief is looking forward to resuming his firm grip on the federation's hierarchy, championing union interests on the Pay Board and, above all, leading labor's 1972 drive to defeat Richard Nixon. Mr. Meany is expected back at his Washington desk in a few days. Despite his December hospital stay after recurrence of an old hernia, he evidently has no notion of retiring. Only lasting physical disability, he has indicated, would impel him to quit.

Nonetheless, his illness has revived Washington speculation that even for durable George Meany, retirement day may come. Premature though it may be, there's talk of possible successors. Among the likelier prospects mentioned are:

—Lane Kirkland, the AFL-CIO's 49-year-old secretary-treasurer who's considered cool, articulate and a bit of an intellectual.

—I. W. Abel, the 63-year-old president of the United Steelworkers, a tough defender of his members' interests.

—And John Lyons, the intelligent and handsome 52-year-old head of the Iron Workers Union, billed as one of a "new breed" of building-trades leaders.

Limitless Authority

No matter who gets the job, the change is sure to be significant. At least to start with, no Meany successor could even approach the power of the blunt-talking, cigar-chomping monarch of the labor combine. He has been its president ever since the American Federation of Labor and the Congress of Industrial Organizations joined more than 16 years ago, and by now, says one man involved in the labor movement, "his personal authority is almost limitless." Moreover, though he might prefer right-hand-man Kirkland, he has avoided openly grooming any successor. Thus Mr. Meany's exit would in itself open up many prospects for change. Among those now foreseen:

—Labor's united front would crack on some issues. On the Pay Board, any Meany successor wouldn't be able to speak for all five labor members; presidents Leonard Woodcock of the United Auto Workers and Frank Fitzsimmons of the Teamsters would feel freer to take an independent line, at least as long as their unions remained outside the AFL-CIO. The union chiefs who sit on the AFL-CIO's 35-member policy-making executive council would begin operating more independently. The jurisdictional strife that's usually confined to Mr. Meany's office—disputes over which union should represent, say, seamen or bus drivers —would be more likely to burst into the open and would be harder to quell.

—In some ways, however, labor might close ranks. Mr. Meany's retirement could speed the return of the ousted Auto Workers and Teamsters to the AFL-CIO; he isn't going out of his way to bring them back in. And the federation would probably give its affiliates more help on bargaining and organizing efforts. Recruiting of white-collar workers might get fresh emphasis.

—Though labor's ties to the Democrats might remain as strong as ever, Republicans would probably see a fresh chance to seek blue-collar support, and so they would woo the new AFL-CIO chief. If the GOP controlled the White House, its strategists would stress the benefits the Teamsters derive from their fairly independent political line; these include easy entree to the White House and appointments to government advisory posts.

—AFL-CIO emphasis on foreign policy would certainly be reduced and there would be a retreat of sorts from Mr. Meany's hawkish, harshly anti-Communist position. Unless lots of jobs were clearly at stake, the AFL-CIO might lobby less vigorously for military projects like the antiballistic missile, which it backed last year.

Some Other Possibilities

Speculation about the post-Meany era is risky because so much hangs on the timing of his retirement. He already has outlasted a number of "potential successors" since taking office in 1955. A 1963 analysis in The Wall Street Journal listed four leading candidates; today one is dead, two have retired as presidents of their unions and the fourth has slipped from the ranks of front-runners.

Even now, a realistic roster of possible replacements must go well beyond Messrs. Kirkland, Abel and Lyons. Other oft-mentioned prospects are Joseph Beirne, the peppery, 60-year-old president of the Communications Workers, and Paul Hall, the 57-year-old president of the Seafarers International Union. Still others can't be dismissed: S. Frank Raftery of the Painters Union, Peter Bommarito of the United Rubber Workers and Charles Pillard of the International Brotherhood of Electrical Workers.

On most lists, however, Mr. Kirkland ranks near the top. He has close ties to Mr. Meany. And while Mr. Kirkland has no dominant union as a base of power (he hails from the tiny Masters, Mates and Pilots Union), he has the advantage of not being too closely identified with either the old AFL-building trades or the old CIO industrial unions—arms that are still occasionally jealous of each other.

Despite Mr. Kirkland's calm demeanor (and his constant use of a cigaret holder) "he is a tough man," asserts one labor insider. Mr. Kirkland first won the respect of some AFL-CIO leaders through his hardnosed but fair efforts to put through a new procedure for solving jurisdictional disputes. That was in 1961, when he was executive assistant to Mr. Meany.

While Mr. Kirkland is sometimes critical of liberal intellectuals, he's veiwed by some union men as something of an intellectual himself. Indeed, his critics cite that bent, plus the fact he never has been elected to any union office except the one he now holds, as possible drawbacks for an AFL-CIO president.

To others, though, one of Mr. Kirkland's main assets is his image of intelligence, restraint and articulateness. "Lane would be a wonderful spokesman," says one insider. "All of you snooty newspapermen would listen to him." Another echoes this theme: "Take The New York Times; they just slap Meany around. Now Lane—he'd get the attention of the intellectuals who write the editorials."

Mr. Abel and Mr. Lyons

In contrast to the AFL-CIO secretary-treasurer, Steelworkers chief Abel boasts a strong power base. He heads the federation's largest affiliate with about 1.1 million members, and he's president of its Industrial Union Department (IUD) as well. He's unassuming and widely respected; he worked his way up through the ranks of his union. Mr. Abel can serve only one more four-year term as Steelworker chief before mandatory retirement. While he might not have a burning desire to succeed Mr. Meany, insiders say he wouldn't mind crowning his career in the top post.

"Abe would run the federation about the way he runs the Steelworkers and the IUD," predicts one observer. In the Industrial Union Department, he has pressed for expanded multi-union bargaining, greater protection against imports and stronger job-safety laws. He's tough: With Meany help, he recently forced the building trades to back down in a bitter clash over the Steelworkers' right to merge with an independent union that includes several thousand construction workers.

The third top prospect for AFL-CIO leadership, Mr. Lyons of the Ironworkers, can also count on wide support. While his union has only about 170,000 members, he's viewed as a candidate that all the building trades would rally behind. Mr. Lyons gets high marks as knowledgeable and articulate. "He really knows the labor movement," says one observer. "He was educated to be an engineer and trained by his daddy (a former Ironworkers president) to be a labor leader."

Mr. Beirne and Mr. Hall

One man long regarded as a potential AFL-CIO chief is Mr. Beirne of the Communications Workers. Innovative and outgoing, he heads a 400,000-member union that has been struggling to cope with the job threat raised by growing automation. Mr. Beirne has been a loyal

Meany backer. But recently he took an indirect slap at the chief's opposition to President Nixon's trips to Peking and Moscow; it isn't clear how this has affected his standing.

Another long-time favorite for succeeding Mr. Meany was Mr. Hall of the Seafarers. But his chances have dropped sharply since his 1970 indictment for conspiring to make illegal political contributions. (Mr. Hall has denied wrongdoing and is awaiting trial.) Still, Mr. Hall could have much to say about who does get the top post. "He has a lot of IOUs out," says one insider, noting that Mr. Hall's husky seamen have often bolstered the picket lines of other unions.

There's little doubt that Mr. Meany could greatly influence the selection of his replacement. Yet associates insist he won't. One reason is that he appears determined to shun retirement. Another is his apparent worry that to begin favoring a successor would make him a lame duck and thus less effective.

So the decision probably will be left to the executive council, and one scenario seen by union insiders goes like this: Several major industrial unions would line up behind Mr. Abel, the building trades would push Mr. Lyons, and jurisdictional animosity would create a deadlock. Mr. Hall, after getting a cool response to feelers for his own candidacy, would get behind Mr. Kirkland, who would prove acceptable to both the building trades and industrial unions.

"Less Rubber-Stamping"

Whoever succeeds Mr. Meany will have to move slowly in making changes, especially if he is elected by a narrow margin. "The guy who succeeds Meany will have to go easy for a while," figures one observer. "Meany exercises a lot of power, but it has taken him years to get to this point." One result: "There will be less rubber-stamping (by the executive council) of the president's decisions," says a staffer at a major union.

One early switch in emphasis would probably come in the foreign-policy area. Mr. Meany's commitment to hard-line anti-communism (he has denounced the Nixon plan to visit China and Russia as "the No. 1 stunt of the No. 1 stunt man of our times") has vastly influenced the federation's position. One reason: Many powerful union presidents on the executive council, lacking deep convictions about foreign affairs, have been willing to let Mr. Meany pursue what one unionist terms the AFL-CIO chief's "hobby."

In the domestic political arena, Mr. Meany's successor will find it hard to loosen labor's moorings to the Democrats and take a more independent stance, even if he leans that way. The anti-Nixon drive already set for this year will work against any detente between labor and the Republicans for a long time to come.

But within the Democratic Party, the AFL-CIO's role could move away from the old "machine politics" to more cooperation with reformers—or so some liberal union officials speculate. Under new leadership, they hope, the federation at least wouldn't clash head-on with reform elements as it did in a recent battle over the chairmanship of the 1972 convention credentials committee.

"Meany was brought up on the 'old politics,'" says one union man. "He's a master of the old politics. It was even old politics that put John Kennedy in the White House. But everything's changing now, and a new guy might operate a little differently."

Coordinated Bargaining

More certain is a stronger post-Meany push for coordinated bargaining, involving several unions that represent workers in a certain company or industry. Mr. Abel, for one, is all in favor; he has been promoting it in his Industrial Union Department. And the federation might do more itself to organize workers, some observers predict.

Almost any new face in the top spot could make reentry easier for the Teamsters, kicked out on corruption charges in 1957, and the UAW, ousted in 1967 during the feud between Mr. Meany and the late Walter Reuther. Mr. Meany helped lead both expulsion moves. Though he has declared during the past two years that the outcasts are welcome to come back, he hasn't wooed them and probably won't.

If anything, Mr. Meany will probably be cooler to the Teamsters' return now that the union's former president, James Hoffa, has had his prison sentence commuted by President Nixon. Before readmitting the Teamsters, the AFL-CIO chief would want proof that Hoffa is completely out of the union's affairs.

Finally, one more change might grow naturally out of Mr. Meany's retirement: Labor's generally aging leadership could give way to new and younger blood. Many union presidents are in their 60s and 70s. The average age of AFL-CIO executive council members is 64.4. But with Mr. Meany retaining the top command at age 77, critics are afraid to speak out on the age issue. After Mr. Meany departs, there could be open debate on the question of how long union leaders should try to hold onto the reins of power.

AN IRON HAND

By Byron E. Calame
Staff Reporter of THE WALL STREET JOURNAL

NEWTON, Mass. — Fifty-nine-year-old Frank Sonsini stands in a corner of the union hall, a snappy fedora atop his balding head. He is here to collect dues and meet informally with members of Local 32 of the Bricklayers Union. Members approach him only when summoned, and when he talks they listen carefully. Sometimes he acts as a father confessor, sometimes as a bantering buddy, sometimes as a counsel and sometimes as disciplinarian. To most members, he speaks English; to some, Italian.

Frank Sonsini is clearly a powerful man. He's so powerful, in fact, that the President of the United States is trying to put some restraints on him.

For Mr. Sonsini is the business agent for Local 32, the man who runs the union. Almost singlehandedly and without a by-your-leave to international headquarters, Frank Sonsini can negotiate a contract or call a strike. When there are jobs to be had, he decides which members can get them. No one joins Local 32 without his approval. He runs the pension and health-care plans. "Frank operates like a king," says an admiring colleague.

Few of the local's 280 members complain. Thanks largely to Mr. Sonsini's tough bargaining—and a strike along the way—their pay of $7 an hour is almost double their wages of 1960. But to President Nixon and some labor experts, Mr. Sonsini symbolizes a prime reason why wages and prices in the construction industry are soaring even though unemployment is high. Local business agents, operating within the industry's highly fragmented bargaining structure, are often so autonomous and so powerful that nobody can control them, not even their supposed superiors at international union headquarters. The patchwork bargaining structure encourages union locals to try to top one another at bargaining time, these experts say, and makes it easier for locals to mount prolonged strikes.

The President's Aim

Indeed, a major aim of President Nixon's new construction industry stabilization plan is to curb the power of business agents. The plan, which went into operation earlier this month, subjects newly negotiated pay boosts to the review of national craft boards and an industry stabilization committee. Increases exceeding 6% a year are to be approved only in special cases, and contracts can't take effect until they have been approved.

There are some 10,000 building-trades business agents around the country. A close look at Mr. Sonsini and the way he runs his local tells a lot about their power and about a collective bargaining system that has been producing pay boosts for construction workers more than twice as large as those received by factory workers

Mr. Sonsini presides over a jurisdiction that covers the Boston suburbs of Newton, Wellesley, Needham and Dover, an area of about 250 square miles. It's bounded by four other Bricklayers Union locals that have contracts expiring at different times. Parts of Local 32's territory overlap with that of other crafts, such as the Painters Union, which have different pay scales and bargaining schedules. (Although some 200 of the 280 members of Mr. Sonsini's union are bricklayers, Local 32 also includes plasterers, cement finishers and a handful of other kinds of workers.)

Several building trades locals in the area bargain with associations of employers, but Mr. Sonsini insists on negotiating Local 32's contract in joint talks with three large contractors. That agreement then becomes the pattern for smaller contractors and outsiders who come into the local's territory to work.

A Lot of Autonomy

Such patchworks of collective bargaining relationships are a major reason for the industry's skyrocketing wages. Mr. Sonsini concedes that "you can do much better for your men" negotiating alone instead of joining with other bricklayer locals in the area to bargain, as some experts have recommended. But he acknowledges that separate local-by-local talks can encourage leapfrogging.

Where the bargaining is fragmented, the business agents possess a degree of autonomy almost unknown to leaders of locals in industrial unions such as the Auto Workers or Steelworkers, which negotiate nationwide pacts with top management. "The president of a UAW local might bargain over where to move the water cooler," observes a contractor, "but he doesn't negotiate wages."

Mr. Sonsini clearly does more than that. He and his "computer" run the show here. "I have this computer," he explains, tapping his head. "Over here (the right side of his head) I crank in the $1.65 (an hour) or whatever I hear San Francisco has gotten, the $1.40 Cleveland got or what Chicago got." He also cranks in other calculations and shrewd estimates: the toll of inflation, for example, work days lost due to bad weather, the cost of a day in the hospital, an estimate of what employers can afford, and —partly a consequence of rising wages—the growing use of labor-saving substitutes for bricks and plastering.

"Then the computer comes up with a figure that's about what I figure we will have to have," says Mr. Sonsini. "I'm usually within a dime or two (an hour) of what we finally get."

Painless Strikes

If Mr. Sonsini doesn't get what he wants, he can urge his members to strike or slow down. Because of the fragmented bargaining, strikes aren't very painful to the local's members.

During a 21-day strike over contract terms in 1963, for instance, the members of Local 32 scarcely felt an economic pinch, he concedes. "Almost all of them got work," he says, merely by driving 10 or 15 minutes to a project under way in the jurisdiction of a neighboring local that wasn't on strike, or by working on nonunion single-family housing jobs. The result: Local 32 won an 18.2% increase in pay and fringes over three years—a hefty boost by 1963 standards.

In addition to his bargaining clout, Mr. Sonsini wields power in other ways. Franchi Construction Co. here charged in a $200,000 lawsuit filed in 1965 that he sparked a weeks-long work stoppage at a large garden apartment project. Neither Mr. Sonsini nor the construction concern will comment publicly on the dispute. But the business agent admitted as part of an out-of-court settlement that his bricklayers had walked off the job and picketed illegally after the contractor had tried to use nonunion plasterers.

"Frank Takes Good Care of Us"

About the only time Mr. Sonsini is subject to any major restraints imposed by his parent union is when a jurisdictional dispute arises with another craft over who should do a particular job. "The international (union) maintains order," he explains, "the same as the Mafia does." But he often settles even these disputes locally, and generally he runs his union with a firm hand.

Mr. Sonsini likes to tell the story, for example, of the union meeting a few years ago when a contract he had negotiated was up for ratification. Some members called for a secret ballot, but Mr. Sonsini whispered to the presiding officer: "Let them stand up, it's not Russia." Only four members stood up to oppose the contract.

Much of Mr. Sonsini's muscle comes from his control over the supply of workers in the area (by limiting the size of the union) and the referral of his members to jobs. Although there are no contractual obligations to do so, many contractors present their personnel needs to him, and he decides which of his members to send to fill them. His decisions are important to contractors and, obviously, to workers, too.

A member of another building trades local who has been around many of Local 32's members on job sites contends, for example, that "Sonsini favors his pets. If guys give him trouble, they may have trouble getting a job." Yet one member of Local 32 avers that "Frank really takes good care of us." And two major contractors who employ Local 32 members praise Mr. Sonsini as being one of the "fairest" business agents with whom they deal.

Mr. Sonsini acknowledges he's building up union membership "at a controlled rate." It would be foolish, he says, to take in enough members to meet the peak needs of contractors—about 400 in October compared to under 200 in February—and then have workers jobless and angry at him during slack times. The

280 members now compare to only 219 when he was elected business agent in 1958.

Unhappy With Nixon Plan

Because of the seasonal nature of construction work, Mr. Sonsini estimates the average member of his local works on union projects the equivalent of only 30 or 35 full 40-hour weeks a year, producing an annual income of $8,400 to $9,800. (He predicts a new state law he helped push for will give his members three to five weeks more work a year by requiring job sites to be protected during the winter.) Some, however, supplement their earnings with non-union work on single-family homes. It's the lack of work during cold weather, Mr. Sonsini and other building trades leaders maintain, that requires construction wage settlements to be higher than those in other industries.

As might be expected, then, Mr. Sonsini isn't happy about President Nixon's new plan. "We can't take the 6% ceiling," he declares flatly. Yet he says he's willing to give the plan a chance.

Mr. Sonsini has other worries as well. The contractors' frequent admonition that the union is pricing its members out of jobs can't be taken lightly, he admits, because of the growing substitution of precast concrete for brick walls and plasterboard panels for plaster. He fears his members don't fully appreciate this trend.

"I bring this up regularly at every meeting to try to educate them," he says, pointing to an office-hotel complex built over the Massachusetts Turnpike here. He explains that because the $14 million project was constructed with concrete, it contained only $70,000 worth of bricklaying and plastering. In contrast, he cites a new $18 million high school being built here with conventional steel, bricks and mortar; the masonry subcontracts total more than $3 million, and he figures they will keep 40 to 50 bricklayers, plasterers and cement finishers busy for a year.

In many ways, Mr. Sonsini's present job (annual salary: about $10,000 and the same as most foremen) is more demanding than the bricklaying he did for 20 years before being elected business agent in 1958. He's at work most mornings by 6:45 and may still be on the telephone setting the next day's job assignments at 11 o'clock that night.

He began a recent day taking phone calls from cement finishers hoping for work and then from a nervous contractor worried that the crew wouldn't show up on time. Visits to two job sites and lunch with a contractor took up the middle of the day. Back in the office, Mr. Sonsini counsels a wife of a member who recently suffered a heart attack on the job; state officials were balking on granting workman's compensation, and he suggested she contact a lawyer.

Despite the recent defeat suffered by a business agent who had held the office in a nearby local for 17 years, Mr. Sonsini professes to be unconcerned about his re-election in 1973. "I don't ever think about it," he says. "The Sword of Damocles will fall sooner or later—it's inevitable." He has had no opposition since he ran for re-election the first time in 1961. "I'm a lot like a father confessor to the guys," he says. "If there were any great discontent, I'd know about it."

TALKING TOUGH

By JOHN V. CONTI
Staff Reporter of THE WALL STREET JOURNAL

HOMESTEAD, Pa.—Raymond W. Andersen just doesn't fit the standard image of a local union leader.

Only 32 years old, he has been a member of the United Steelworkers of America for not quite five years. As a former appliance repairman, furniture store manager, prison guard, nightclub bartender and car salesman, he isn't exactly steeped in either union or steel-mill tradition. He dresses for local union meetings not in workers' garb but in a silver-gray, double-breasted suit and a shirt with his initials monogrammed on its French cuffs. In his comfortable union office, there's a small executive-style refrigerator and the standard manuals of the self-making man: "Principles of Management" and "Use the Right Word."

Yet Ray Andersen is the new president of USW Local 1397, whose 7,000-plus members toil at U.S. Steel Corp.'s big mill here, right across the murky Monongahela River from Pittsburgh. And if Ray Andersen doesn't fit the stereotype of a local union boss in a mill town, it's partly because the stereotypes are crumbling. A gradual but significant change is taking place in the makeup of big unions like the Steelworkers, and in the men emerging to lead them.

Ray Andersen illustrates a new breed of local union leader suddenly thrust into power in the big-mill locals of the USW. Ambitious and aggressive men in their late 20s, their 30s or their early 40s, these new leaders share with their younger constituents a set of concerns and attitudes toward the union and their jobs that differ vastly from those of the Steelworkers of a generation ago.

An Unpredictable Element

These men, and the pressure on the union brass that they represent, are a force to be reckoned with at the steel bargaining table this year. Their militancy helps explain the unusually demanding posture adopted so far in advance of bargaining by USW President I. W. Abel and his fellow officers. Quick to challenge traditional union policies as well as the foreman's judgment, and eager to swing their new-found weight in the union, the new local leaders and their followers add a new, unpredictable element of instability to steel labor relations.

They aren't an insignificant group. In last year's local-union elections within the USW, an unexpectedly large number of leaders of the largest mill locals were ousted from office, replaced by younger, militant challengers such as Mr. Andersen. Frankly posing as a maverick who would be unbeholden to the union hierarchy, Mr. Andersen won the presidency of his big local on his first try for union office.

The story is much the same at other large steel locals. Militant presidents have newly taken charge of locals at such huge operations as U.S. Steel's Gary, Ind., and Fairless Hills, Pa., works, Bethlehem Steel's Sparrows Point, Md., mills, and Jones & Laughlin's Pittsburgh and Aliquippa, Pa., works.

New presidents at these big mills represent about 70,000 men, or about a fifth of the 350,000 workers at the nine big steelmakers who jointly will negotiate a new contract this summer to replace the pact expiring Aug. 1.

"The Young Challengers"

The new leaders are proud of their difference from the old guard of the union. "Today the reason the younger men are taking such an active part in the union is because they can see more, they can comprehend more," asserts Mr. Andersen. "They don't accept things like the old-country people did. They're a challenging group: the young challengers. You've seen a lot of TV programs—like "The Young Lawyers" and The Young This and Young That? Well, we are The Young Challengers."

Steel company executives are aware of the atmosphere in the union fostered by the young challengers and their militant constituents. "The political pressure in the union is much tougher" now, says an industry negotiator. "Nobody is sacred anymore. There's no John L. Lewis or Philip Murray left" to command unswerving allegiance from underlings.

The new local leaders expect and demand greater respect from mill foremen, both for themselves and their members. They challenge traditional union policies. Currently, for instance, many are pressing for the right to call local strikes over grievances, a practice forbidden by the USW contract and feared as much by top union leaders as by management as a step toward labor chaos at the mills. Some, like Mr. Andersen, also want to change the union's major bargaining strategy so that it would strike only one target company—U.S. Steel—rather than the whole steel industry to win a pattern contract.

The emergence of the new leadership is a product of the steadily changing character of the union's membership. The 1.2-million member USW, the nation's third largest union, takes in about 190,000 new members each year. About one-fourth of the workers in the nation's steel mills have put in five years or less on the job. Nearly half of the USW's basic-steel membership is new to the mills since the last industrywide strike took place in 1959. Until recently, these men have known only labor peace, general prosperity and steady work.

Spreading Attitudes

It has been clear for some time that restlessness and anti-incumbent attitudes have spread through the USW. In the union's top-officer elections in 1969, a practically unknown union staff lawyer named Emil Narick shocked incumbent chief Abel by winning 41% of the vote for union president. At the same time, several veteran district directors of the union who supported Mr. Abel were ousted from office.

Thus the new elements of political pressure within the union that have surfaced since the last round of steel bargaining are likely to influence the negotiations this year. Some of the young leaders already talk of mounting a

grass-roots challenge to the union's top leadership in 1973 should the Abel administration fail to deliver the big contract gains it has promised for 1971.

In the union's steel industry conference, meantime, the rebels' voices are likely to be heard loudly. The conference is made up of local union presidents and has the power to ratify or reject any bargain made by the top USW officers with the industry. The 1968 steel settlement negotiated by Mr. Abel was nearly defeated in the industry conference—in an atmosphere generally considered to have been less militant than that prevailing today.

The militancy of the Steelworkers' rank and file can't, of course, be attributed only to the young members and their new leaders. "There's no question that all our guys are being hurt, both financially and spiritually," says one USW district director. But it is the younger workers, lacking seniority and earning lower wages, who are hurt the most by inflation, layoffs and other economic characteristics of the times.

Naturally More Vocal

"In times of high inflation," comments one steel company labor-relations executive, "the young guy who's trying to bring up five children, make payments on his house, buy furniture and so on is going to get hit harder than the guy who's 55, has his kids raised, has the better job in the mill and gets paid more. Naturally, the younger guy is going to be more vocal."

Industry and union observers say these younger, more vocal union members exhibit a new set of attitudes shaped by the increased affluence of their times, the higher level of their education, their increased mobility and all the new expectations that these influences combine to create. They expect more and they demand more from both their jobs and their union.

Articulating their feelings, Homestead union chief Andersen talks in terms that might be used by today's college students fighting for identity in huge universities or young men trying to find a place in a giant corporation. "We're not just a check number, we're human beings," says Mr. Andersen. "We have on-the-job needs and off-the-job needs." He talks about "finding out where better relationships are going to come from"—relationships with the company, the foreman, the union leader.

Mr. Andersen contends that employers don't fully appreciate the changes he represents. "They aren't dealing with a bunch of buffoons or oafs or fools," he says. "They are dealing with some serious people around here who take their work serious. I take this job serious," he says.

Chafing at Discipline

The newer mill hands chafe more at supervision than did their elders, often leading to conflicts over discipline. Harry Piasecki, 35-year-old president of a 16,000-man Gary local, says the number of company disciplinary actions in his local are running about twice what they did five years ago. Mr. Andersen asserts that the 800 men in the open-hearth furnace shops at the Homestead Works received no less than 285 written disciplinary notices in the space of four months last year.

The disciplinary problems and the day-to-day grievances of the workers are major factors behind a volatile issue in the union: the right to strike on the local level during the term of a contract. Currently, such strikes are banned. To settle grievances, workers and their local leaders must use a complex, five-step grievance procedure that ultimately leads to arbitration; most local leaders consider the process complicated, costly and overly slow. They want a faster remedy for grievances: the strike. "If we had the right to strike," says Mr. Andersen, "we'd have something the company would listen to. Now they're laughing at us. Right down at us."

Steel executives shudder at the thought of the stop-and-go production that could result from constant local-issue walkouts; USW chief Abel also contends that local strikes could cause chaos. The industry and the union already have a joint study team trying to find ways of improving the grievance-handling without resorting to local strikes.

Mr. Andersen and some of his local union colleagues differ with the union hierarchy on another matter, too: its bargaining strategy. Rather than picking one company as a strike target and concentrating on winning a pattern settlement there—as the United Auto Workers does in bargaining with car makers—the Steelworkers' union leaders prefer to negotiate with the industry's nine-company bargaining committee and strike all the companies at once if necessary.

Grand Talk of Strategy

"I'd like to see them take on U.S. Steel," says Mr. Andersen. He reasons that a strike against the No. 1 producer, which accounts for about one-fourth of domestic production, would hurt the economy less, reduce chances for federal intervention and permit still-working members at the other companies to support the strikers at U.S. Steel by special dues assessments. "Then we could bend these companies into shape," he says with relish. Despite some pressure for such a change, USW leaders appear likely to hew to their traditional strategy this year.

Though he grandly talks of bargaining strategy now, it wasn't long ago that Mr. Andersen was drifting from one job to another. Then five years ago when he decided to marry he quit his job tending bar in New Kensington, Pa., to take "more steady" work in the Homestead mill. There he took a job as a pipefitter, a craft he still practices periodically in order to maintain his seniority and fringe benefits as a U.S. Steel employe. He makes about $9,000 a year, he says, the average wage for a pipefitter in his seniority class. The union makes up any mill wages he loses when working on union business.

"I just attended my monthly meetings, things went so fast, and here I am today," he says, musing over his rise to local president. But it's obvious from observing him on the job that he worked at getting to his present position and he's working to go higher; he talks of someday becoming one of the union's 24 district directors, or maybe even president. "It would take a lifetime of devotion," he says.

...AND JOE MOLONY REMEMBERS THE PICKET LINES

By MICHAEL K. DRAPKIN

Samuel Gompers may well have enunciated the labor movement's guiding principle —'More"—but for 36 years Joseph P. Molony of the Steelworkers, an Irishman of impish wit and glib tongue, has surely helped refine it.

Once, during the bitter copper strike of 1967-68, a company negotiator suggested he might add a few cents to the wage offer—if only Mr. Molony could get the miners to eat their lunches underground.

"And what'll you be givin' me," the union man replied in his soft, measured brogue, "if I can get 'em to *live* underground?"

For Joseph Molony, who grew up in the famine-ridden Ireland of a half-century ago, and who helped organize the Steelworkers in the face of company police atop the mills with machine guns, "More" has never been defined as money alone.

First as an organizer, then as district director and finally, for the past eight years, as vice president of the United Steelworkers of America, Joe Molony has always stressed the other concerns of his members—the working man's status as a man, the safety of his work place, his ability to buy a decent home and to send his kids to college.

Now, after years of speaking with great authority in the inner councils of the nation's second-largest industrial union, Mr. Molony reaches the mandatory retirement age of 65. Pausing over a cup of coffee at a Pittsburgh hotel the other day, he could sum up his views of the labor movement—past, present and future—very simply as "the last, best refuge of the poor."

That's not a fashionable view today, when much of the public castigates organized labor for a range of real or fancied ills. The unions often are seen as the epitome of the greed that fuels inflation, as bastions of racism and corruption, as harboring a public-be-damned attitude, and for their authoritarian internal rule.

But those weren't the concerns of Joseph Molony and his compatriots of four decades ago. They worried, instead, about the basic wage rate in the unorganized steel industry—47 cents an hour—and the unconcealed hate with which management greeted the Steelworkers Organizing Committee (SWOC), headed by Philip Murray, an organizer on loan from John L. Lewis and his United Mine Workers.

"At first the issue was recognition, not money," Mr. Molony recalls of those days in the 1930s. Franklin Roosevelt and the National Labor Relations Board helped settle that issue. "We probably all would have failed but for F.D.R. and the Board," said Mr. Molony. Typically, he credits the late President, rather than his union's organizing efforts, for bringing "the industrialists to heel."

Progress was slow in steel, but then U.S. Steel Corp., the industry leader, stunned other companies by granting SWOC a contract in 1937. The rest of the steelmakers, known collectively as "Little Steel," took a strike for more than a year. SWOC failed to crack them then, but by 1942 all the big steel producers had recognized the union.

Mr. Murray sent Joe Molony to organize

deck hands on the ore boats working the Great Lakes. Then when the USW was formed out of SWOC in 1942, Mr. Molony became its director in New York State, a post he held until 1965 when he teamed up with I. W. Abel, his friend and ally, to challenge the leadership of then USW President David J. McDonald.

As a $42,500-a-year vice president, Mr. Molony has been a perfect counterpoint to Mr. Abel, a skilled administrator and negotiator. It's been Mr. Molony and the excitement that his speeches can generate that Mr. Abel has called on to rally rank-and-filers to the union cause, be it approval of a dues increase or ratification of a hard-won contract.

Invariably, those speeches have a reminiscent tone, recounting past struggles and ultimate triumphs. Today Mr. Molony can speak of "deadly dull" days on the picket lines, but at a Steelworkers convention his tales of the same event sparkle with meaning and purpose.

It troubles Joseph Molony that so many people don't share his enthusiasm and, in fact, have a negative attitude toward organized labor. People think "we take great glee in mucking up the system, that we have supreme power, that we use the strike weapon with abandon," he says. "Of course, none of that is so."

Rather, he says, there's the great faith on the part of most unionists in capitalism as a system. "It's put more goods in the hands of more people than any other," he says. But it's the unions, he believes, who've made the system work. "Capitalism never was worth a damn, except to a handful of millionaires—until the unions came along."

To make the system work, it takes militancy and, yes, occasionally even a strike, Mr. Molony suggests. While there hasn't been a strike in the steel industry since the record 116-day walkout of 1959, Mr. Molony is wary of suggestions that the USW lay aside its chief economic weapon. "The right to abstain from work is something we can't surrender," he says resolutely.

Such economic pressure has served well in the past, he says, and continues to be useful today. Thus as the nation turns from an industrial to a service economy, the labor movement should follow. "If I've a harsh word for labor today, it's not that it's cozying up to Nixon. After all, you've got to live with the people who are in power. It's that we aren't organizing fast enough." Only 25% of the nation's work force is unionized, he notes.

Thus, Mr. Molony applauds the efforts of militant young labor leaders like Victor Gotbaum of the Municipal Workers and Jerry Wurf of the Government Employes, who, he feels, are seeking the same goals he sought in those early days.

"They may be dealing with a new era, but they're asking the same questions we asked," he says.

Looking up from his cup of coffee, he waves his arm in a wide arc. "You can throw a stone from where we're sitting and hit people making lousy wages. These people need a union as badly as I needed one 36 years ago."

But it's a special kind of unionism he's calling for, a kind that believes strongly in the working man. Unions "have to be big and strong," he says, "and, above all, honest."

But they need another element as well. "You can hire lots of smart guys to run your union, but to do the job you've got to have compassion."

That's the kind of union man Joe Molony of the Steelworkers has been for more than four decades.

II. COLLECTIVE BARGAINING

The primary activity of American labor unions has always been and continues to be collective bargaining with respect to compensation, hours of work, and other conditions of employment. This activity of course affects not only the welfare of workers but also many management functions and how they are performed, and, indirectly, the character and condition of the economy. Thus, the importance of collective bargaining cannot be overemphasized.

Since 1935 collective bargaining has been regulated by the National Labor Relations Act (the Wagner Act). This law was enacted in order to give employees the right to organize and bargain collectively. In 1947 the N.L.R.A. was amended by the Labor-Management Relations Act (the Taft-Hartley Act), a law which in turn was amended in 1959 by the Title VII of the Labor-Management Reporting and Disclosures Act (the Landrum-Griffin Act).

The National Labor Relations Act, as amended, spells out the rights and obligations of both employers and labor organizations. This law is administered and enforced by the National Labor Relations Board, an independent federal government agency which performs both prosecuting (i.e. enforcement) and judicial functions. The general counsel of this agency is its chief prosecutor and a presidential appointee, while the judicial functions are carried out by a five-member board whose members are also appointed by the President. Inasmuch as the decisions of this board have a tremendous effect on the application, interpretation, and enforcement of the law, it is obvious that the character of collective bargaining in the United States is very much affected by the fact that these board members are political appointees. The first article in this section, "Washington Shift," describes the changes in the membership of the Board which took place a few years ago as a direct consequence of the election of a Republican administration in 1968 and points out some of the significant implications of this change.

The best-known aspect of collective bargaining involves the negotiation of a collective bargaining agreement. Although management may and usually does submit bargaining proposals, negotiations tend to be primarily concerned with the demands of the labor organization. These demands tend to reflect to a considerable extent the needs and wishes of the union members. An example of such demands and how they were developed is provided by the second article in this section, "A Day's Work," while the next article in this section, "The 'Me-Too' Union?" compares how two major labor organizations dealing with the same industry prepare for contract negotiations. Of course, unions ordinarily ask for higher pay; however, as is illustrated by "Bitter Choice," once in a while workers are willing to accept a cut in their wages if such action appears to be necessary to preserve their jobs.

Labor organizations in the public sector, whose membership and power have increased substantially in recent years, often make demands which involve basic policy decisions. "Who's in Charge?" provides an interesting insight into such demands, why they are made and why they are opposed by government officials.

If contract negotiations do not result in an agreement, the members of the union may and frequently do strike. "Hitting the Bricks" points out that, in recent months, the number of strikes has been increasing and that this increase is largely attributable to the double-digit inflation which has plagued the economy and reduced the real earnings of workers. The basic idea of the strike is that it hurts both the employer and the employees and, thus, puts economic pressure on both parties to resolve their dispute and reach an agreement. However, as is shown in "Striking the Modern, Painless Way," striking workers do not always suffer real economic hardships and, consequently, may not feel any great pressure to make concessions and achieve an agreement.

Strikes often have long-lasting effects, as illustrated in "A Loss of Markets." Moreover, almost all walkouts affect not only the employer and his employees but also others who are not a party to the labor dispute; a good example of this is provided by "Who's on First? Who Cares?" which describes the effects of the 1972 strike of major league baseball players.

Throughout the history of the United States, it has been illegal for government employees to engage in strikes. In recent years, however, as "Big John's Dilemma" illustrates, pressure has been mounting to grant employees in the public sector the right to take such action; in fact, in some instances government workers have gone on strike even though this conduct was clearly illegal.

While public employees have been trying to obtain the right to strike, a number of efforts have been made to reduce or even eliminate walkouts as a weapon in collective bargaining. " 'Best Offer' Arbitration's Critics" explains one interesting suggestion that has been tried in a few instances in recent years. Another widely-publicized effort is the 1973 agreement between the steelworkers union and the major steel companies which is discussed in "An End to Bargaining Cliff-Hangers?." Whether or not this attempt will be successful and will spread to other industries is, at this point in time, difficult to predict. However, an indication of what may happen is provided by Australia's famous arbitration system, a somewhat similar approach which has been in operation for many decades and is described in "Defiance of Everything."

The grievance process is widely recognized as the heart of collective bargaining. The basic reason for this is the fact that the day-by-day handling of grievances determines, more than anything else, the overall quality of the labor-management relationship within an organization.

The union representative who is primarily responsible for the handling of grievances, at least in the initial stages, is usually known as the shop steward or grievance committeeman. An excellent description of what the duties and activities of this union official may involve is presented in the first "On the Line" article, while the second "On the Line" article presents an interesting example of the functions and responsibilities of his management counterpart, the foreman.

How many grievances are submitted depends, of course, on many factors such as the specific provisions of the collective bargaining agreement and the history and character of the labor-management relationship. Frequently, the number of grievances tends to increase prior to contract negotiations and, as "Edgy Employes" explains, during periods of declining economic activity.

If a grievance is not resolved through the grievance procedure, the issues involved are usually presented to an arbitrator, a neutral third party whose job it is to decide the case, a decision which is ordinarily binding both on the employer and on the union. In the last few years, however, as is illustrated in "The Final Work," some labor arbitrators have started to take a somewhat different approach in their efforts to resolve labor-management disputes. This new approach, if it should be widely adopted, can be expected to have a considerable impact on the future development of collective bargaining.

What about the future of labor relations? In this age of change, it is of course difficult to predict with any degree of certainty what will happen in the years to come. At the same time, it is important to recognize that there are some clues which provide an indication as to what may happen. Among these clues are those which involve practices and developments in other countries. For example, Australia's arbitration system which is discussed in "Defiance of Everything," an article mentioned above, involves an approach to the settlement of labor disputes which for many years has had considerable influence on the thinking of American labor relations experts. Other illustrations of foreign developments are contained in "The Worker's Voice," an article that describes the German system which permits workers to participate in management decision-making, and in "By the Book" which explains a relatively new union tactic that has been tried by workers in both England and Germany. Of course, labor relations in the United States differ in many ways from those in Europe and other parts of the world; therefore, it is doubtful whether these foreign practices will ever be widely adopted in this country. And yet . . . .

WASHINGTON SHIFT

By Elliot Carlson
Staff Reporter of The Wall Street Journal

WASHINGTON—Union men are finding it tougher sledding once again at the National Labor Relations Board.

Accused of a pro-labor bias during its 10 years of Democratic domination, the board has begun to shift ground now that it has a Republican majority. It's hewing closer to lines generally favored by employers, putting more obstacles in the path of union negotiators and organizers—though it hasn't yet upset any landmark decisions favoring labor.

"We may be moving back to a period where employers could get away with anything," contends Stephen Schlossberg, general counsel of the United Auto Workers. "They'll be able to make all kinds of threats against workers trying to organize and scare the pants off them." Union people generally claim the board had a pro-employer bias during Eisenhower days.

The board's Republican chairman, Edward B. Miller, has been in office for 10 months, though the five-man board has had a Republican majority only since January. It already is getting high marks from the U.S. Chamber of Commerce. For the most part, the board's recent decisions "represent a favorable turn," says Anthony J. Obadal, the chamber's director of labor relations. But Mr. Miller and his majority get failing marks from unions. "Miller doesn't appear to be very sympathetic toward workers," says Mr. Schlossberg. He cites as one example the chairman's deciding vote last year against a severe new remedy sought by the UAW against an employer that had long refused to negotiate.

Mr. Miller

Two Terms Expire Soon

Labor's disaffection is expected to deepen this summer, when the terms of two Democratic officials expire. The first, in June, is that of Arnold Ordman, who, as general counsel but not a board member, decides whether to issue unfair labor practice complaints to be heard by NLRB examiners. The second, in August, is that of board member Gerald Brown, long an object of employer wrath. The replacements are expected to be more conservative.

But the changes aren't enough to placate all the board's conservative critics in Congress. Republican Rep. John Ashbrook of Ohio, still professing grave doubts that the board decides cases fairly, recently proposed that it be replaced by an independent labor court.

There's dissatisfaction, too, among liberal Democrats. On Thursday a House Labor subcommittee led by New Jersey Rep. Frank Thompson begins hearings that will, among other things, review the board's performance and consider legislation aimed at strengthening remedies available to aggrieved workers.

Clues to the NLRB's future course under Mr. Miller may be provided in a number of pending cases. One issue is whether the NLRB should decide disputes where contractual arbitration provisions haven't been exhausted. Another deals with the extent to which employers may refuse to recognize union authorization cards and demand an election. Finally, in a widely publicized case involving a Texas farm cooperative, the NLRB is grappling with whether racial bias in hiring and promotion constitutes an unfair labor practice.

Debate About the Mission

Critics say that if the NLRB decides to defer to arbitration provisions this would indicate a board less likely to intervene in tough union-employer disputes. What's more, "there are signs the Miller board will be much less innovative in extending employe rights" against employers, says Theodore J. St. Antoine, a professor at the University of Michigan law school.

A case in point, he says, was Mr. Miller's vote last year against a UAW demand that Ex-Cell-O Corp., a Detroit machine-tool maker, reimburse employes for wage boosts allegedly lost by its refusal to bargain. The board unanimously agreed the company's refusal was illegal, but it ruled 3-to-2 that the NLRB lacked authority to order such an unusual remedy. (An appeals court later disagreed; the NLRB is seeking Supreme Court review of the case.)

Denying any pro-management bias, the 49-year-old Mr. Miller contends he simply interprets the job differently from Frank McCulloch, his Democratic predecessor. "Frank felt the board had a social mission over and above just interpreting the law," explains Mr. Miller, a soft-spoken, reflective man who before his appointment was a lawyer for managements in Chicago. "My view is that the NLRB should be as much as possible like a court, without any social or economic objectives."

To show his impartiality, Mr. Miller says that under his chairmanship the board has continued some controversial McCulloch-board trends, such as extending NLRB jurisdiction to new sectors of the economy. To professional baseball, nonprofit colleges and nursing homes and private hospitals, the Miller board has added orphanages and homes for unwed mothers and now is considering extending coverage to employes of law firms.

Moreover, employers harbor reservations about some Miller-board decisions, such as a unanimous ruling ordering General Electric Co., in certain circumstances, to turn over to three Electrical Workers Union locals wage information confidentially gathered for bargaining purposes.

Less Venturesome

Nonetheless, the Miller board generally is expected to be less venturesome than its Democratic predecessor. The old board had ruled that employers had to assume the labor contracts of predecessor firms, for instance, but the Miller board recently held that under some circumstances, an employer isn't bound by a predecessor's labor contract.

Yet even its severest critics don't expect the Miller board completely to overturn landmark rulings. For one thing, the courts have affirmed so many past decisions that the most rambunctious board couldn't upset existing precedents. For another, such activism would be out of character for the new chairman.

Rather than fashion radical new remedies, the chairman believes the board simply should intervene less in local labor disputes. This view has shown up regularly in his opinions. Basically, Mr. Miller would allow both employers and unions in representation elections "a wider latitude of speech," would intervene less frequently in cases where there are accusations of failing to bargain in "good faith" and would demand more convincing proof to support charges of unfair labor practices.

A DAY'S WORK

By Laurence O'Donnell and
Walter Mossberg
Staff Reporters of The Wall Street Journal

DETROIT—Complaints about life on the assembly line are going to land on the bargaining table next summer when the United Auto Workers union begins negotiations for new three-year contracts with General Motors Corp., Ford Motor Co. and Chrysler Corp.

Most demands will probably focus on escape from the job—through a shorter work-year or improved early-retirement schemes—rather than on changes in the job itself, the system of in-plant discipline or the nature of the assembly-line process. UAW leaders are skeptical that there are any easy answers to complaints about assembly-line work.

However, they may seek changes in the contracts to give workers, as a matter of principle, some say over the pace of their work and their immediate work environment. They may also ask that outside consultants be used to determine and evaluate job-enrichment experiments.

While none 'of this may seem revolutionary, there are strong indications that the whole thrust of making "the job" a bargaining issue will be vigorously opposed by the auto companies. To be sure, the companies themselves have in certain instances instituted a variety of experiments aimed at making life on the assembly line more pleasant and meaningful for workers, while at the same time boosting productivity. Chrysler, for example, under the direction of Group Vice President Eugene Cafiero, is testing a number of plans to further "involve" its line employes in the production process.

Hands Off Please

But the companies view these experiments as their own purview and regard some of the union's proposals, including the right of workers to accept or reject overtime assignments, as a fundamental assault on the companies' rights to manage. Other proposals to give workers more time off, or to shorten workers' careers, are viewed as costly, inefficient and a basic threat to recent company drives to cut labor costs and improve productivity.

Richard C. Gerstenberg, chairman of General Motors Corp., highlighted this concern in a New York speech earlier this week. He warned that public sympathy for factory workers, based on "misconceptions," may result in rising labor costs—and rising consumer prices. The public, he said, doesn't realize that shorter work-weeks and greater worker control over tasks "almost all involve an extra cost—a direct cost to the manufacturer which must inevitably be reflected in the price of the product; that is, the price the consumer must pay."

Nevertheless, "the job"—and such matters as more time off and more say from workers—will receive higher priority than in earlier rounds of bargaining for several reasons. For one thing, UAW leaders are casting about for demands that have wide appeal but aren't tied directly to wages. They presume that the UAW will probably be bargaining next year under some sort of wage controls—and will thus be restricted on the size of wage increases.

Growing Pressure

Perhaps more important, UAW leaders are under growing pressure from their members to make escape from the job a high priority issue next year. One grass-roots group, claiming the support of 20 Detroit-area locals and backing from "hundreds" of other locals across the country, wants the work-week reduced to four nine-hour days with workers paid the same amount for 36 hours as they get currently for 40 hours. To discourage weekend work, Friday pay would be time-and-a-half; Saturday, double-time; and Sunday, triple-time. (Workers currently get time-and-a-half for almost all work beyond 40 hours a week, except Sunday when they get double-time.)

"The time you have to spend at work is all out of proportion with the time you have left for your family and yourself," says Frank Runnels, president of Local 22, who is chairman of the four-day work-week committee. "In the old days the concept was that a man's whole life was built around his job. Now he's not willing to sell himself into industrial prostitution."

Another group, centered in Flint, Mich., and viewed as a powerhouse within the union, is pushing for major improvements in the early-retirement plan the UAW won in 1970 bargaining (the plan allows workers with 30 years in the plant to retire at age 56 with a $500 a month pension). To make early-retirement more feasible, the national "30 and out" committee wants a $650-a-month pension with a cost-of-living escalator clause and no minimum-age restrictions.

The Central Issue

Complaints about working conditions will also be the central issue, as they have been in the past, in next year's local-contract bargaining. Each plant has its own contract covering special problems, including air-conditioning, heating, location of drinking fountains and space for union activities; this contract expires at the same time as the national agreements. As part of these local negotiations, which often lead to crippling strikes even when strikes over master contracts are averted, the local seeks to resolve grievances stemming from disciplinary layoffs and other worker complaints. Since many workers at General Motors plants are angry over the company's efficiency moves, troubles are expected next year over local contract talks at some GM facilities.

The UAW isn't waiting for next year's bargaining to cope with the problems of job unrest. Earlier this year, it asked Ford to enter into a joint study of assembly-line boredom and drudgery and consider ways to shorten the work-year. It also asked Ford to give workers the day after Thanksgiving off because overtime schedules have been heavy this fall. The union went to Chrysler to ask for a voice in the job-enrichment programs the company has undertaken.

All these efforts, however, have been resisted, prompting UAW leaders to believe they are in for a tough battle next year. Ford turned down the holiday bid and agreed only to "study the propriety of studying" assembly-line monotony and a shorter work-year. Chrysler met with the union but hasn't given it a voice in its experiments.

Actually, there is no organized pressure from the UAW's rank and file to overhaul the assembly line. "Nobody has ever come up to me and asked the union to help enrich his job," says Douglas Fraser, vice president of the union in charge of its Chrysler department. He adds: "If you asked me how to humanize the plants, I couldn't tell you how to do it." Many UAW leaders concede that most workers, given the chance to change their jobs, probably wouldn't.

Nevertheless, Mr. Fraser and others believe the union should push for more experiments to see what could be done. And those experiments, Mr. Fraser says, should be handled by outside consulting firms. The use of outsiders, he believes, would solve the problem of management picking the experiments without union consultation and then drawing its own conclusions.

Mr. Fraser is critical of the fact that Chrysler began its job enrichment experiments unilaterally—without consulting the union. Some union leaders have also complained privately about worker experiments at GM and Ford that are being run by the companies—again without union consultation.

Ken Bannon, the UAW vice president who runs its Ford department, believes absenteeism would drop and quality would improve if workers had more control over the pace of their work, instead of having the speed dictated by the pace of the assembly line. By being allowed to get ahead of the job, workers would be able to create extra relief time so they could have an occasional "smoke break, or visit with their neighbor," Mr. Bannon says. (Assembly-line workers at Ford get 46 minutes off during each eight-hour work-turn, but they must stay at their work station unless specifically excused.)

Mr. Bannon plans to push for a clause in the master contract that would recognize, for the first time, that workers as a matter of principle should have some say over their job—how it is done, the pace of work—leaving details to be worked out in local plant agreements. UAW officials, however, expect both proposals to be strongly opposed by the auto companies as infringements of company rights.

Concerning time away from the job, most union leaders currently favor some system that would shorten the work-year through longer vacation periods. One plan being seriously considered would credit workers for hours worked, allowing them to build up a bank of points, rewarded with a paid week off. While this plan would require the auto companies to have more workers, the vacations could be staggered over the year and thus avoid big fluctuations in manpower.

Although the short work week is popular with many workers, the idea is currently viewed coolly by top leaders of the union, who note the double cost to the companies—heavy overtime costs in peak production periods, plus the cost of unused facilities.

UAW leaders are also sour on "voluntary overtime" as a priority demand next year. Though it is talked about by the rank and file and Mr. Fraser says it could be the "real sleeper demand" of 1973, he and others in the UAW command are fearful it would take a strike to win. The auto companies claim they need to be able to order mandatory overtime during peak production periods and would have to hire replacements for regular workers when too many opted to take Saturdays off. Company officials wonder what they'd do with those replacements when regular workers opted to work.

The companies also fear regular workers could, in effect, strike in the event of a grievance by deciding not to show up for overtime work. "I don't know how to operate this business if everyone wants to say when, where and if he will work," says Sidney McKenna, director of Ford's industrial-relations staff.

Mr. McKenna also echoes a view widely held among the auto companies when he adds: "There is very little evidence—in fact, none that I'm aware of—to suggest that a reduction in working time will increase employe satisfaction while at work."

THE 'ME-TOO' UNION?

By ROY J. HARRIS JR.
Staff Reporter of THE WALL STREET JOURNAL

ST. LOUIS—When Aluminum Workers International Union delegates met here and representatives of the United Steelworkers Union gathered in Pittsburgh recently to plan for the contract talks they're currently holding with major aluminum producers, their respective headquarters staffs helped shape the demands.

With a sophistication that befits the nation's largest industrial union, the USW distributed 100-page computer printouts detailing provisions in its 91 individual contracts in aluminum and packed with data on areas where it felt improvement was needed. Members were told, for instance, that "successor clauses are found in 40 agreements covering only 39.2% of the employes." Such clauses, which protect an employe's rights when a plant is closed or sold, should be provided in all agreements, the USW said.

But delegates to the Aluminum Workers meeting were handed only a collection of letters submitted by the locals themselves. So they learned of the desire by workers in Corpus Christi for an 18% wage increase and of interest in Baton Rouge in a shortened workweek. There was no computer printout because the union has no computer. In fact, the AWIU isn't even sure it could adopt such hardware to the rank-and-file brand of democracy its members prize. "What do you put in a computer if the members say, 'Go to hell' " on a contract issue? asks Lawrence A. Holley, the union's research director.

Seat of the Britches

The USW, 1.4 million members strong and representing numerous industries, overshadows the 35,000-member Aluminum Workers union in more ways than one. (The USW even has 20% more members in the aluminum industry than does the AWIU.) While the Steelworkers can draw on a skilled staff of eight researchers, and operates out of a 13-story Pittsburgh office building, Mr. Holley says he and his one assistant work "by the seat of our britches" from the AWIU's small downtown St. Louis office.

A top negotiator for one aluminum company, who asks not to be identified, says such differences are clearly visible at the bargaining table. The Steelworkers' bargaining sophistication "shows up right away in terms of its financial capability," he says.

The USW research team, headed by Otis Brubaker, a former economics professor, pursues such highly technical areas as supplemental unemployment benefits, pension formulas, wage escalators and earnings-maintenance provisions. By contrast, the company negotiator says, the Aluminum Workers concentrate on one question: "How much do I get?"

Every three years the peculiar differences between these two unions are highlighted as they separately seek their common goal of improved pacts with Aluminum Co. of America, Reynolds Metals Co. and Kaiser Aluminum & Chemical Corp. The aluminum labor scene has particular interest as bargaining resumes in New York today after a holiday recess. By prior agreement, the two unions and the "big-three" companies have advanced talks by four months and set a Feb. 1 target date for a settlement, replacing the usual cliff-hanging negotiations when the contract expires on May 31.

In addition, all sides have agreed that any unresolved issues will be submitted to a top-level labor-management committee for settlement. All this is an attempt to reduce the fear of a strike that leads to stockpiling by aluminum buyers. The aluminum workers figure 10% of the industry work force was laid off after the current contract was signed in 1971 as customers worked off the bloated inventories they had laid in while negotiations were in progress.

Patterns for Steel

Further, the aluminum package is bound to set patterns for the USW's negotiations with the basic steel industry beginning Jan. 30. In fact, the advanced bargaining date in aluminum is a by-product of the Steelworkers' "experimental negotiating agreement" with steelmakers, which attacks the far more serious stockpiling threat in that industry by completely barring the prospect of a nationwide steel strike.

Thus, to an extent the Aluminum Workers union is following the USW's lead. If the precedent of prior years prevails, both unions will sign nearly identical contracts. (An effort was made to break the pattern in 1968, when AWIU members struck for two months after rejecting a contract offer that had been accepted by the USW. The USW contended, however, that the eventual AWIU contract was only a "face-saving" compromise containing no important concessions by aluminum companies.) But AWIU members resent any implication that they belong to a "me-too" union that blindly follows the lead of their "big brothers" at the USW. Members take a fierce pride in their union and claim their methods, rough-hewn though they may be, give them a close feel for the human problems in the plants that may be obscured by a larger union's statistics.

Roots in the 1930s

Vernon E. Kelley, executive assistant to Henry E. Olsen, the Aluminum Workers president, shrugs off the "me-too" label by telling how AWIU officials shot down at least one major Steelworker goal in their early discussions on the advanced bargaining plan. The USW sought a "no-strike" clause similar to the one it had signed in steel. But that requires compulsory arbitration, which "we didn't want," Mr. Kelley says. As a compromise, both sides agreed on meetings between the union presidents and company chief executives as a backup for a Feb. 1 impasse. The big aluminum producers went along with the "summit-meeting" provision, which was written into the final agreement revealed last August.

The Aluminum Workers traces its origins to the first efforts in 1932 to organize five plants run by Alcoa, which back then *was* the aluminum industry. While the AWIU was chartered by the American Federation of Labor, the USW entered the aluminum industry in the mid-1930s by absorbing locals established when the forerunner of the Congress of Industrial Organizations formed its own aluminum union. The dual representation wasn't altered when the AFL and the CIO merged in 1955.

A look at how policies and demands are drawn up underscores a key difference between the unions today. The USW relies mainly on investigative visits by its staff men to the plants. Their reports form the basis of the computerized analysis. In contrast, Mr. Holley, the AWIU research director, says the Aluminum Workers don't know "which way we're going to go" in negotiations until letters arrive from the locals.

When actual talks begin, AWIU negotiators regularly consult the local unions in a painstaking procedure to weed out less-important demands. And unlike the USW, which delegates to representatives at an industry conference the power to approve a contract, the AWIU takes its package back to the locals for ratification. "They have the power to say yes, no or go to hell," Mr. Holley says.

This year the presence of government controls and the industry's rather weak profit performance in recent years are dampening labor's contract hopes in aluminum—at least compared to 1971. One company negotiator suggests that pay increases may be close to the annual 6.5% to 7% accepted in other industries. And Mr. Olsen, the AWIU president, cautions members in private "not to expect as big a settlement" as the 31%, three-year package won last time.

There are hints, however, that new ground may be broken in some noneconomic areas.

BITTER CHOICE

By Jim Hyatt
Staff Reporter of The Wall Street Journal

AKRON, Ohio—William Yakubik's union and his boss have been talking about wages, and Mr. Yakubik doesn't like the direction the conversation is taking.

"They want us to take a pay cut and I can't see that. That's going backwards," insists Mr. Yakubik, a tire builder and a 31-year veteran at a Firestone Tire & Rubber Co. plant here.

Wage cuts? With inflation still driving prices upward? That's the theme Firestone is pushing here as the key to bringing new rubber industry jobs to town. Last month, the company wrote Local 7 of the United Rubber Workers that in order to locate a new radial truck tire plant here, a longer work week and a lower hourly wage rate would be necessary. "We can locate at any number of places at wage rates at or below Akron rates," says J. V. Cairns, Firestone's vice president-labor relations. "The union wanted to know what would have to be done to increase our capacity in Akron, so we told them."

Wage cuts are usually an explosive topic for any management and any union. But the squeeze on productivity has forced many employers these days to raise the issue openly at last as one way to save jobs and avoid layoffs. Perhaps more significantly, some unions are responding to the idea with less than absolute horror. Reluctant as they might be to consider such an idea, they figure work at a reduced wage is better than no job at all.

Joining the List

In recent months, such diverse groups as taxi drivers in Cleveland, paper mill employes in New York, and watchmakers in Pennsylvania have taken pay cuts, some on a temporary basis. Now there's talk of wage-cutting among many of the 11,000 hourly workers at General Motors Corp.'s Frigidaire division in Dayton. It's still too early to call wage-cutting a trend. But both union officials and corporate labor experts in a number of industries concede that if the economy stays in the doldrums, they may be forced to join the list of businesses that have already whittled pay checks.

Even some union officials themselves are adjusting their own wages due to financial problems. At the United Auto Workers, more than 800 international representatives have volunteered to delay until next January a 7% wage increase that would have been effective Aug. 1.

Wage cuts in industry can affect employes at all levels ranging up to the executive suite, where cuts may be felt either as outright pay reductions or as reduced bonuses as profits evaporate. Usually, in fact, it's easier to cut executive and white-collar salaries than it is production-line salaries.

In some instances, at least, the cuts are only temporary. For about four months recently, some 2,000 salaried employes of Wheeling-Pittsburgh Corp. took a 10% pay cut, a move executives said made a "significant contribution to the well-being of the corporation." The money was restored in February. In late 1970, executives and key employes at Warner & Swasey Co., the Cleveland machine tool concern, took pay cuts of up to 35%. Chairman James C. Hodge received aggregate remuneration of $100,000 in 1969, but only $86,577 in 1970, according to proxy materials.

While no less painful, achieving pay cuts for hourly workers is considerably more difficult. Hourly rates usually are set by lengthy contracts, and changes require approval by often skeptical rank-and-file union members. "The union leader who proposes a pay cut is putting his head on the block," says one corporate labor relations official.

A Suspended Cab Bonus

Nonetheless, in cases where the employer pleads economic distress, such agreements can be worked out. Cleveland taxi drivers in June voted to reduce their pay by giving up a bonus of 5½ cents a trip. The bonus had been won during 1966 negotiations. Yellow Cab Co. said it was losing money and would restore the bonus once profitable levels are reached.

In Lancaster, Pa., about 2,000 salaried and union employes of Hamilton Watch Co. agreed to a 10% pay cut during the first half of this year to conserve cash. And in one widely noted instance, about 450 employes of Wear-Ever Aluminum Inc., the cookware subsidiary of Aluminum Co. of America, voted last year to forgo wage and fringe benefit increases during the third year of a contract. John S. Hamilton, president of the Chillicothe, Ohio, concern, says that, partly as a result of the move, operations by year end "could be close to a profit for the first time in many years."

In Mechanicville, N.Y., a group trying to reopen a shut-down paper mill, formerly operated by Westvaco Corp., has asked workers to accept a new contract providing for a 10% pay cut and reduced benefits. The 550-man union local was "very co-operative and receptive to the plan," says an official of the new management group, called M-7 Papers Inc. The new management had argued that the mill couldn't be economically reopened unless wages were cut. The mill is slated to reopen next month.

Wage cuts proposed by less financially troubled concerns, however, often put union leadership on the defensive. With Firestone's wage proposal, grouses one union leader in Akron, "the company wins either way." He theorizes that if workers turn down the lower hourly wage rate for the new plant, the company can make the union the scapegoat for taking the jobs out of town. If the union accepts, of course, the company secures the lower rates without moving.

Thus one political faction of Local 7 at Firestone has been handing out leaflets labeling the wage cut, and other rubber company proposals to improve productivity, as "a nationwide conspiracy" and an effort to "break the chain of union strength."

Firestone specifically seeks to establish a new job classification called Radial Tire Assembler. The worker would be paid $5 an hour for five eight-hour days a week. At present, tire assemblers work a six-hour day for six days a week and make $6.14 an hour. The company insists that overtime under the new arrangement would bring average earnings near the present level. Because workers would put in more hours, there would be one less work turn daily.

The other major rubber companies are also seeking to change work rules and to institute the eight-hour day. Simply changing shifts four times a day loses much work time, they insist. (Some proposed changes are a little more unusual. B.F. Goodrich Co. is seeking to pay workers by check instead of cash, a practice the other tire companies abandoned several years ago. One worker explains that B.F. Goodrich employes like to be paid in cash so they can throw away the pay envelope and squirrel away a few dollars before handing the money over to the family.)

Firestone's proposed new truck tire operation is only the tip of the controversy, the union asserts. At best, only a few hundred workers would be employed at the new venture, at least in the beginning. The union worries however, that the company soon will try to spread the lower rates to other, already-existing jobs. "We can't put ourselves in a position where we'd buy a pig in a poke," says Local 7 President G. D. Gelvin. "We would insist any negotiations be pointed specifically at radial truck tires and not at the rest of the plant."

On such a limited basis, however, he says the union might consider the proposal. And some workers agree. "We want the production in Akron," says tire builder Julius Garman, 49. "Without a guarantee that the jobs will stay in Akron, it puts us behind the eight ball."

At some companies, it's difficult even to get the idea of a wage cut officially on the table. At Dayton, for instance, officials of GM's Frigidaire division have bluntly said that without vast, dramatic improvements in productivity, the appliance business' future is bleak. But in "state of the company" talks to workers, Vice President and General Manager Harold W. Campbell has stopped short of suggesting a wage cut. "GM is a proud company," says one observer close to the situation. "They aren't going to get down on their knees and beg."

Still, company officials pointedly note that Frigidaire pays electrical workers as much as $2 an hour more than competitors such as General Electric Co. and Westinghouse Electric Corp. And as a result, down on the assembly line and in the general community, prospects of a pay cut are the number one topic of conversation.

"Pray, Pray, Pray!"

An ad hoc "Committee to Save Frigidaire for the Community" has asked in newspaper ads for suggestions on how to do so, and many of the 1,200 responses have called for a wage freeze or cut, says Frank G. Anger, head of the committee and chairman of Winters National Bank and Trust Co. "A retired man from Frigidaire wrote in saying he had just received a $22-a-month increase in his disability pension," Mr. Anger says, "and he said he'd be glad to give it up. Another person, who didn't work at Frigidaire, said he's willing to take a cut and buy a major Frigidaire appliance. A senior citizen wrote in: "Pray, pray, pray!""

Such talk, of course, has the union at Frigidaire, Local 801 of the International Union of Electrical Workers, on the defensive. "They've got public opinion to the point where we're the bad guys," moans Joe Shump, president. Still, he recalls, "we signed our contract last Nov. 23 and there was no indication then they couldn't choke down the package." Frigidaire pays wage rates comparable to those negotiated by the United Auto Workers at GM's auto plants.

Mr. Shump himself last Monday suggested reopening contract talks between Local 801 and Frigidaire as a way to get the situation "off dead center" after announcing that he plans to resign soon and become Ohio's state industrial relations director. Mr. Campbell of Frigidaire says, "We are willing to talk with the union" on the matter of new negotiations.

A little over half of Frigidaire's 11,000 employes in Dayton do appliance work. The others build auto air conditioning compressors. More than 3,100 appliance workers at the plant have been laid off in the last year, and another 126 are due to be laid off today.

Refusal to Open Books

Making a convincing case for a wage cut at Frigidaire may not be easy, despite the community uproar. The company won't say whether its appliance business is profitable, and adamantly refuses to open its books to the union. Without such information, Mr. Shump insists, the union wouldn't know how big a wage cut would be needed to save jobs.

Mr. Campbell, the general manager, will only say that "our competitive problem is very serious. The other appliance manufacturers have a big competitive advantage." He admits Frigidaire has investigated such alternatives as subcontracting work outside of Dayton, moving elsewhere, and even building appliances in Japan.

Some Dayton observers are convinced GM originally planned to move Frigidaire out of town or even cease appliance manufacturing entirely until such movements as the "save Frigidaire" committee evolved. The Dayton business community is deeply concerned over the prospect of losing Frigidaire, which started work in the city more than 55 years ago and which in 1970 produced its 70-millionth product.

In any case, labor relations experts view the Frigidaire situation as highly significant. Rising imports, they assert, will put a similar wage squeeze on other manufacturers sooner or later, and the resolution of Frigidaire's wage dilemma could set a pattern for other employers.

Well, Maybe a Little Cut

Some Frigidaire workers already say they would consider a wage cut if one were absolutely necessary. "When another raise comes up in September, most are willing to forget about that one," says Fred McKenzie, 47. "I wouldn't mind a little cut—not more than a dollar an hour," adds Doug Limes, 29, a refrigerator assembly line worker.

Still, other union men view wage cuts as sheer "union-busting" tactics. "They're trying to put fear into the working man so he'll submit," asserts cigar-chewing Tom Miller, a union representative at Frigidaire. "They want the union to take credit for screwing up the deal," adds another Frigidaire worker, a veteran of 27 years.

Among the unions that have agreed to cuts elsewhere in the nation are construction trade unions, whose large wage settlements previously have symbolized the nation's wage spiral. Union electricians near Cleveland have agreed to trim rates for work on one and two-family dwellings by $4 an hour, or about 50%, to stimulate home building and generate jobs. In Pittsburgh, the building trades council and Mellon-Stuart Co., a large commercial builder, have agreed to a one-year, 10% wage cut and reduction of double-time and overtime provisions for some work.

"I put the cards on the table and they were totally in agreement," says R. N. Peters, executive vice president of Mellon-Stuart. "They wanted to be part of the market, and could see the writing on the wall that nonunion people were getting a larger share of the market. It's better to have a percentage of the market than none at all." Some crafts in the area are 45% unemployed, and the agreement should lead to more work, agrees an official of the building trades-council. The agreement might even be extended beyond one year, he adds.

Some workers are finding they can exchange a wage cut for other job improvements. In Middletown, Ohio, the teachers association in May approved a one-year contract with no salary increase in exchange for reduced classroom sizes. The school system had tried to keep classroom sizes under 30, an official says, but wasn't always successful. Under the new contract, some classes will have as few as 18 students, and most will be in the 22 to 24 pupil range.

WHO'S IN CHARGE?

By ALLAN J. MAYER
Staff Reporter of THE WALL STREET JOURNAL

Who's in charge, anyway?

Should teachers set policy for the schools? Should social workers help set welfare standards? Should policemen have a voice in determining the size and deployment of the police force?

Those are tough questions, and there are no easy answers. But those are the questions that state, county and local governments and their employes are wrestling with this bargaining year. For as the wages, hours and working conditions of these organized public employes greatly improve, their unions, particularly those of professionals, are attempting to broaden the scope of negotiations to include policy questions that used to be the exclusive province of elected officials.

The elected officials are putting up resistance.

"Control and power are the guts of this year's demands" by New York schoolteachers, says David S. Seeley, director of the Public Education Association, a citizens group in New York. "Who is going to run the schools and make the decisions, the United Federation of Teachers or the representatives of the public?"

"No One Tells Doctors"

More than four million of the nation's 13.5 million government workers belong to some union, and the number is growing rapidly. And as the unions grow, so do their goals. "There isn't anything that the 43 unions we deal with are ashamed to come in and bargain about," says Allan Davis, Detroit's chief labor negotiator.

Each side makes some potent arguments.

"To the professional — the teacher or the case worker—things like class size and case load become as important as the number of hours in a shift is to the blue-collar worker," says Victor Gotbaum, executive director of District Council 37 of the American Federation of State, County and Municipal Employees. The council represents 90,000 city employes in New York.

"No doctor would let a hospital board tell him what kind of knife to use when he's in the operating room," says David Selden, president of the 275,000-member American Federation of Teachers. "It's the same thing with many public employes. There are questions of professional integrity involved." The UFT in New York is affiliated with the AFT.

The rise of public-employe unions has occurred over the past 25 years, largely in the past 10. Virtually every gain made by these unions sets a precedent because there is still little legislation anywhere in the country clearly defining what should and should not be negotiable. Hence there is widespread interest in the current New York teacher negotiations.

The Federal Level

(On the federal level, it is mostly clerical and blue-collar workers who belong to public-employe unions. Consequently, these unions' impact on public policy at this level is just about nonexistent. There are no federal laws concerning collective bargaining with federal employes, but legislation defining policy in this area has been introduced in Congress.)

Thirty states have laws mandating that governments must bargain with all public-employe unions. These laws typically say that the governments must negotiate "wages, hours and conditions of employment." Only rarely does the law specify matters that shouldn't be negotiated. And even where statutory limits do exist, they are often of little help, says John Hanson, director of personnel for Hennepin County (Minneapolis) Minn., because "conditions of employment can be interpreted pretty broadly." Just how broadly is a central issue in the current New York talks.

The teachers asked for, among some 700 other things, smaller classes, a "no layoff" policy, uniformed guards in the schools and a $2-million-a-year Educational Development Fund "to support research and experimentation in areas of professional concern and provide training for new teachers."

The UFT's president, Albert Shanker, freely concedes that some of the demands had policy implications. But, he insists, "what we're primarily interested in is improving the teachers' working conditions." It just so happens, he adds, that "there is hardly anything which cannot simultaneously be viewed as a working condition and a matter of educational policy."

Size of Classes

The issue of class size is one of Mr. Shanker's favorite examples. "You can approach it from the point of view of what's best for the children or as a question of allocating resources," he says. "But, obviously, handling a lot of kids is more difficult than handling just a few. And in that way, it's most certainly a working condition."

Mr. Seeley of the Public Education Association says he is amenable to the notion that teachers should have some role in shaping education policy. But he insists that it would be a mistake to "lock it into a contract." Mr. Seeley dismisses the teachers' argument that if doctors, through their medical associations, can control medicine, then teachers should have the same right to control education. He argues:

"While doctors may control medicine, the client usually has his choice of practitioners. With education, the public school is usually or effectively the only game in town."

But Mr. Seeley adds that his major objection is a philosophical one. No one group, he says, should control the schools "because education is a public institution and we're supposed to be a self-governing people. We haven't yet succumbed to rule by experts."

Replies Mr. Shanker: "These things aren't philosophical questions. To the extent that teachers are attacked for the failure of the schools, they must be given a voice in how those schools are to be run."

This feeling of responsibility is shared by public employes elsewhere. Nurses in Milwaukee County's public hospital system are de-manding improvements in health care for patients; corrections officers in Connecticut, Maryland and New York have included prison reforms in their contract demands; police in Spokane insist that the city hire more patrolmen.

And in New York ("This sort of thing always seems to start there," says a spokesman for the National League of Cities' Labor-Management Relations Service), welfare case-workers are fighting recently established "work-fare" programs under which welfare recipients must accept government jobs. "The whole thing smacks of slave labor," charges a spokesman for District Council 37, which represents New York's case-workers. "They're making welfare clients work for $1.90 an hour at jobs that were previously done by case-workers at $3.50 an hour. So there's an element of job security for our members involved, too."

Case-workers in Milwaukee have taken a similar stand and are fighting, as are their counterparts in New York and Minneapolis, to establish limits on their case load.

This push for greater employe participation in policy-making is confined almost exclusively to the public sector because, according to a recent Labor Department study, management in private industry has a defense: It can argue "that it is primarily accountable to the stockholders from whom it receives its authority, and that managers need the flexibility to respond to new conditions quickly and surely to meet the competition." In the public sector, the study says, "there is no exact parallel to this argument."

The same study says that conflict over the scope of negotiations for professionals "can be viewed as a struggle for power between professionals and the administrator." The professionals, it indicates, seem to be gaining the upper hand.

"I'm convinced that labor groups, minority groups, disadvantaged groups, everybody in the country is out to get some piece of the decision-making action," says Ray Wesley, chief labor negotiator for Spokane. "And in many ways I think that's a healthy thing." But he adds: "When a union seeks to wear the mantle of management by insisting on having a say in policy at the same time it wears the mantle of labor, then it doesn't understand its role."

And so when Spokane police attempted to get the city to hire more patrolmen, the city refused even to bargain about it. "As far as we're concerned," Mr. Wesley says, "that's a matter of city policy."

Also opposed to any union control over public policy is Arvid Anderson, director of New York City's Office of Collective Bargaining. "Should we let police decide how to deal with the narcotics problem?" he asks. "Or should we leave it to the social workers?" His view is that "all of them are entitled to an input, but the questions we're involved with should have a broader constituency than just an employe relationship."

"I would expect public-employe organizations to have a say in how their departments are run whether or not there is such a thing as a collective bargaining mechanism," Mr. Anderson says. "Whether by picketing city hall or writing to their councilmen or availing themselves of the media, they can make their influence felt. But I draw a distinction between that kind of input and saying, 'We have a right to determine how this should be, and if you don't go along we'll go out on strike.' "

It isn't always that simple, however. In Milwaukee, for example, county social workers objected to a plan that would have changed their work schedule from a five-day, one-shift work-week to a six-day, two-shift week. The union couldn't force the county to bargain about the new policy of staying open six days a week, but it could avail itself of a recent state law that said that while policy isn't negotiable, the impact it has on working conditions is.

So, says Robert G. Polasek, chief negotiator for Milwaukee County, "we'll be forced to bargain over the reassignment of shifts, overtime pay and the like." And the effect of this, he says, will probably be the same as if the union had been permitted to bargain about the policy in the first place.

This type of law is common. And many public-employe unions seem happy with it, perhaps realizing that it can give them some control over policy.

"We aren't asking for the right to declare war or determine whether there should be a welfare system," says Mr. Gotbaum of District Council 37. "The system is already here. All we are saying is that within the system there are certain procedures which affect employes in how well they can do their jobs. And it's what those procedures are that we would like a say in determining."

HITTING THE BRICKS

By James C. Hyatt
Staff Reporter of The Wall Street Journal

WASHINGTON — Surging inflation and the demise of wage controls are reviving labor's ultimate weapon: the strike.

From bakers in Massachusetts to nurses in San Francisco, from teachers in Wisconsin to household movers in Pittsburgh, strikes big and small are spreading through a wide variety of industries.

Work stoppages in the nation's offices and factories dipped dramatically in 1972 and 1973, when labor unions found generous pay pacts difficult to squeeze past federal pay controllers. Indeed, the 27 million work days lost to strikes in each of those years was the lowest total since 1966.

Since May 1, however, the bargaining handcuffs have been unlocked. And with the consumer price index in April up more than 10% from a year ago, unions are reaching for all they can get. They want not merely to catch up, but to get ahead of inflation if possible. Cost-conscious employers are balking, of course. The end of controls has created an unsettled new bargaining atmosphere in which none of the old formulas seem to apply.

The Frequent Result: Stalemate

In other days, union bargainers typically sought higher pay to reflect productivity gains and to keep pace with cost-of-living increases. Given inflation's pace during the past year, wage boosts would have to exceed 10% a year just to enable workers to keep up, compared with last year's 5.8% average wage boost for major contracts. But productivity, which historically has been rising at about 3% a year, plunged 5.5% in the first quarter, the steepest decline since 1947. Reduced output per hour of work, in turn, aggravates unit labor costs and makes employers more adamant about holding down wages.

More and more often, the result is stalemate at the bargaining table, followed by a strike.

The first hints of growing labor unrest surfaced in March, when 430 work stoppages began, the largest total for any March since 1937. In April, nearly twice as many workers hit the bricks as a year earlier. And while May figures aren't yet tabulated, the Federal Mediation and Conciliation Service finds itself watching "more labor disputes than we've been in for 15 years, by a wide margin," a spokesman says. As of June 6, FMCS mediators were trying to resolve 523 strikes involving 308,-600 workers; the total excludes hundreds of smaller strikes as well as disputes involving public employes.

"We'd Like Some, Too"

A sampling of the current disputes:

A walkout June 1 by 110,000 men's-clothing workers was the first industrywide strike since 1921, with cost-of-living protection a major issue. "Our members are the victims of soaring inflation and low wages," insists Murray H. Finley, president of the Amalgamated Clothing Workers of America. Yesterday the union membership approved a proposed settlement ending the strike.

Electric-utility customers in the 10,000-square-mile territory served by Pennsylvania Power & Light Co. are having their bills estimated, because 5,000 meter readers, installers, clerical workers and power-plant operators are on strike. The walkout, the first at the utility, also turns on the cost-of-living issue. After all, the utility can adjust billings as fuel costs increase, notes Earl J. Wenner, chief negotiator for the Employees Independent Association. "They like this protection and we'd like some of it, too."

Thousands of construction-trades members have walked off billions of dollars worth of projects in Philadelphia, Cincinnati, Denver, Syracuse and Memphis; they're exercising their bargaining muscle for the first time in three years. And a number of trades are winning pacts worth twice the Nixon administration's old 5.5% wage guideline. At last count there were 137 strikes in construction.

At Harvard University, 40 bookbinders and lithographers who normally work in the printing shop have rejected a 5.5% wage offer and are now busy passing out handbills assailing the well-endowed university. "Only $1.3 billion in the black," reads one flier. "Fight on, Harvard. Maybe you can make even more." The workers belong to the Graphic Arts International Union.

A Bump in the Road?

To be sure, rising joblessness could temper some strike fever later this year. Unemployment, 5% in April, rose to 5.2% in May and is expected to rise further the second half of this year.

Moreover, federal officials have other reasons to hope that strikes will calm down later this year. "We expected an upsurge in strikes following the end of controls, and we had one," says W. J. Usery Jr., director of the Federal Mediation and Conciliation Service. But he notes that the number of expiring building trades pacts drops from 916 in May to 660 in June and a scant 170 in July.

"What we're going through now is like a bump in the road," suggests another federal labor observer. "We're waiting to see whether it is going to stop traffic."

For now, though, there's little sign that the militancy of workers will diminish soon. Union leaders unanimously blame inflation for spurring the new walkouts. "For the last two or almost three years, an economic strike has been in effect a strike against the government," says Richard Prosten, research director for the AFL-CIO's Industrial Union Department. Such strikes proved "very difficult," and unions "delayed and deferred strikes until they appeared to be more fruitful," he says. "I guess now is the time. Inflation has eroded everything. These people are really dying."

Federation President George Meany sounded the same theme last week in a speech to the Retail, Wholesale and Department Store Union convention. He assailed "two-digit inflation that eats away at your members' paychecks like a flash fire." And he added: "Workers know when they are getting an 'expletive deleted.' "

Labor officials have long insisted that only wages were effectively controlled during the wage and price controls. They note that real spendable earnings of workers—paychecks adjusted to reflect Social Security and federal income taxes and the effect of inflation—were 5.6% lower in April than a year earlier. And April was the 13th consecutive month that such year-to-year comparisons have declined.

The Bureau of Labor Statistics finds that a typical factory worker with three dependents had real spendable earnings of $99.74 a week in April, compared with $107.93 in April 1973. This was just 52 cents a week more than real take-home pay a full decade ago.

At the same time, the fact that corporate profits have stayed firm isn't lost on the unionists. The Commerce Department says that these after-tax profits, adjusted for inflation, rose 15.8% in 1971, 12.8% in 1972 and 21.5% in 1973.

"I've seen some fairly decent offers (from management) that two or three months ago would have been gobbled up," says a researcher for one major union. "Now, people are turning them down."

The Machinists Union tabulated nine wildcat strikes in a recent two-week period, more than usually occur in a full six months. And airline mechanics in the union have voted down settlements with two airlines, seeking improved contract terms. "We are seeing the outrage our members feel at being victims of a national economic policy," says William W. Winpisinger, a vice president of the union.

"There's no question strike activity has picked up," says Gilbert Jewell, president of the Milwaukee-based Allied Industrial Workers. "We've got six or seven strikes in effect at the present time. And I don't see anything that anybody's doing that's going to change the situation. As long as inflation keeps going, a man has to try to defend his position."

Other unions also expect strike activity

to increase. The half-million-member Service Employes International Union has had "some very narrow settlements, coming right at the 11th hour" says organizer John Geagan. "There will be more strikes" if inflation continues its costly pace, he warns. "When you hit them in the market basket, our people just can't take it."

Regardless of the size of eventual settlements, of course, strikes prove costly to the parties and disruptive to the economy; prolonged shutdowns aggravate shortages and often cost manufacturers sales that can never be regained.

Fruehauf Corp. officials estimate a 12-week shutdown by the Allied Industrial Workers Union at a brake plant cost the company $5 million in lost profits earlier this year. Workers at Cessna Aircraft Co. went to shortened four-day weeks in April when a strike at a supplier curbed delivery of airplane engines. A six-week strike by stove workers at a Tappan Co. plant probably "cost us about 10 cents a share in earnings," says W. R. Tappan, chairman and president; it was the first strike at the firm's Mansfield, Ohio, plant in 93 years.

Workers at one of the nation's longest continuing major strikes may find some of their jobs gone when the dispute eventually is settled. Some 7,200 Whirlpool Corp. workers went on strike at an Evansville, Ind., division Feb. 17; they are members of the International Union of Electrical Workers who make refrigerators, upright freezers and window air conditioners. The lengthy dispute is hung up over fringe benefits. But in late May, even as the dispute continued, Whirlpool officials said one assembly line employing about 1,000 workers in Evansville is being dismantled and will be moved to Fort Smith, Ark.

There are plenty of other chances for bargaining unrest this year; more than 5 million workers are covered by major collective bargaining agreements expiring or reopening in 1974. Yet-to-be negotiated pacts involve communications, aerospace, railroad and nonferrous metals. The gloomiest prospects loom for the coal industry, where hoped-for early talks between coal operators and the United Mine Workers haven't yet started. Dwindling coal stockpiles make the prospect of a coal strike particularly worrisome.

STRIKING THE MODERN, PAINLESS WAY

By David Gumpert

LYNN, Mass.—"We regret the heavy costs of the strike to so many. Everybody has been hurt by it. Employes on strike lost more money than they may ever recover, and General Electric may never make up its lost earnings."

With that traditional employers' post-strike statement, General Electric Co. drew the curtain last week on the nationwide walk-out that had closed its plants for 14 weeks. There seems to be a question, though, to what extent this traditional statement any longer applies. Whatever the strike's effects on GE, many of the 130,000 or so strikers just didn't suffer all that much. At least here in Lynn, an old and fairly typical GE community located 10 miles outside of Boston, GE's statement simply rings hollow.

Lynn's economic life continued nearly un-affected by the strike, no easy task consider-ing that 12,000 workers were on strike. Of course some of the effects are still to be felt in the form of accumulated debts and post-poned mortgage payments, and the strike's impact may have been more severe in other GE communities where conditions were dif-ferent. Workers throughout the Boston area, especially, have been enjoying the benefits of a tight labor market. Yet what happened here in Lynn says a lot about striking under to-day's economic and social conditions.

"If you came here looking for hardship cases, you'll have trouble finding them," an editor of one of Lynn's daily newspapers re-marked as the strike was being settled last week. The president of the Lynn Merchants' Association, Morton Zonis, observed, "We all expected to be clobbered at Christmas and in-stead we went ahead of last year." And Janu-ary was about normal for retailers for this time of year, he added.

Economy Almost Unaffected

Lynn's economic fortunes suffered little for the simple reason that most of the 12,000 GE strikers had alternate sources of income during the strike. About 2,500 received be-tween $65 and $110 a week in welfare. The vast majority of the remainder found full-time or part-time jobs or else had wives who worked. The bulletin board at the Interna-tional Union of Electrical Workers Local 201 in Lynn was filled with notices seeking elec-tricians at $6.60 an hour and welders and burners at $3 and $4 an hour. Appeals for temporary bus drivers and for men to deliver telephone books went unfilled as many strik-ers took their choice of jobs.

Jack Nabozny, a GE tool and die worker for the past 29 years, is a case in point. Dur-ing the last three weeks of the strike he was earning $52 a day helping clean up pollutants accidentally dumped in a nearby river. In ad-dition, his wife had earned $54 a week as a temporary saleswoman in an area depart-ment store for the strike's duration. And for pocket money, the 60-year-old Mr. Nabozny received $20 a week for picketing GE's River Works plant in Lynn. He didn't run up any debts during the strike and he even managed to continue providing money for one of his children in college. "I did well this strike," he observes, a contented smile crossing his full, weathered face.

Mr. Nabozny, however, can remember a time when he didn't do so well, for he was in-volved in GE's only other lengthy national strike—a 9-week walkout in 1946. "I had a lot of-soup-then,"-he-recalls.-"I had four kids in grammar school and I couldn't pay my rent. I was lucky because my landlord let me wait till the strike ended, but I bet I lost two or three years trying to get myself back to where I was before the strike started."

Others who were around during the 1946 strike like to compare that situation with the just settled strike. "It was like the bottom fell out," says Harry Zimman, owner of Zimman's Inc., a Lynn department store, of the 1946 dispute. "There were no jobs available then. If a guy came into my store during this strike and asked for a job I could find a place for him. In 1946 there was nothing here or anywhere."

Mr. Zimman's business dropped by about one-third during the 1946 strike—this time it was "about even with the year-ago period." Whereas in 1946 people stopped buying the clothing necessities like shoes and pants and underwear, this time the only sign of hard times Mr. Zimman noticed was "we didn't see as many $20 bills as we ordinarily see."

Jim Donahue, a vice president of IUE Local 201 and a veteran of 46 years with GE as a tester, points out that the current economic situation made things a lot easier for union organizers. "This time there were no calls here at the union of people wanting to go back to work like there was then," he says. "After a few weeks in '46, the people had pretty much had it."

Even the union's own provisions to strikers have improved markedly during the intervening 23 years. In 1946, the most a striker could expect from the union was soup lunches and food and medical aid in cases of dire need. During this strike, the union provided complete hot lunches and $20 a week for those that picketed.

The simple fact is that going on strike today is not the great personal sacrifice it once was. What happened in Lynn and probably in other GE communities this strike around was that workers suddenly discovered that they had a variety of financial alternatives in lieu of GE. The usual strike situation, where the company sits back and lets the workers take it on the chin for a while before a settlement is reached just did not apply in this situation.

Better Paid Jobs for Some

Lynn's workers went on strike expecting the worst but instead they found that today's prosperous middle-class-oriented society was prepared to take care of them and in some cases reabsorb them in more attractive ways.

Robert Comeau, 29, a GE iron worker, made this discovery early in the strike. A slightly built bespectacled young man, he had been with GE for nearly five years prior to the strike and was earning $3.85 an hour. During the second week of the strike, however, he was hired by a neighboring company at $5.25 an hour to do nearly the same work "with no questions asked." He was also receiving his $20 weekly picket money.

By strike's end, he had purchased a color television set, paid off some long-standing furniture bills, and was in the market for a new car and house. And he was faced with the pleasant task of deciding whether it was in his interests to return to GE. Indeed, there are indications that one of the main reasons a settlement was reached when it was, with GE giving more than it originally intended, was that the company suddenly realized that if it didn't settle soon it might have considerably fewer workers left when it finally did settle.

The experience of Mr. Comeau and others like him has ramifications beyond its impact on GE and the final settlement. It shows not only that jobs were plentiful, but also that they were open to strikers, an important change, since not long ago hiring strikers was completely taboo, in the interests of employer solidarity. Some of Lynn's strikers reported resistance on the part of employers to hire them once they knew they were with GE, but for every refusal there were other offers of either temporary jobs or else permanent jobs extending beyond the strike.

And along with the change of attitude among employers, the workers benefitted from a basic change in attitude toward strikers by the general public. James Fuller, 68, a retired GE worker who was on strike in 1946, remembers public antipathy as another burden along with the financial problems. "In those days you were an outlaw if you went on strike," he says. "Then the only person who helped you was the corner grocer who knew you over the years. To other people you were a socialist. I had some pretty bad names yelled at me on the picket lines then." He credits the mass media with changing the public view of strike situations these days.

Additional evidence of the public's changing attitude toward strikers in the Lynn area was the ease with which strikers were able to cash in on welfare. A family only had to have less than $1,000 in savings to qualify. And a law to provide unemployment benefits to strikers, which is in effect in New York and Rhode Island, was only narrowly defeated in the Massachusetts legislature a few days before the strike was settled. In the 1946 strike, the old-timers recall, one had to be virtually destitute to be able to receive any public assistance.

For Robert Thomson, a burly 18-year veteran with GE, the $80 weekly welfare payments added to his $20 picketing money meant he could devote a lot of time to union activities during the strike. The money didn't go as far toward supporting his wife and six children as the $136 a week he took home when he worked and he had to defer part of his mortgage payments for the strike's duration.

And when things looked bleak at Christmas for the Thomson family, that symbol of middle class opulence—the Master Charge credit card—came to the rescue. "I did all my Christmas shopping on that," he says, adding that he hasn't yet received the bills for the $400 worth of merchandise he purchased then.

Another Time, Another Place . . .

A wide open job market, public assistance, union wealth and easy credit all helped transform the GE strike from an act of bitter last resort to a relatively painless next step in the negotiating process. Not all of these factors would apply in every strike or at every time, of course; the tight labor market here may not persist forever. Even so, it's obvious that times have changed since the days when the heavy-damage-to-all-sides statements first became traditional, and that the ease of striking has its effect on the balance of power in labor negotiations.

When GE workers look back on the winter of 1969-70, they may wonder that the whole thing was as painless as it was. They suffered, but that kind of suffering could give them visions of holding out for even more the next time around.

A LOSS OF MARKETS

By James Carberry and James E. Bylin
Staff Reporters of The Wall Street Journal

Most West Coast businessmen may be sighing with relief at the apparent settlement of the prolonged Western dock strike, which has been costing the California economy alone about $17 million a day.

But a number of companies that ship through West Coast ports now are worrying about a serious and long-lasting problem created by the strike—the permanent loss of business and markets it had taken years to cultivate.

"It's as simple as this — some customers who leave don't come back, or don't come back immediately," says Donald Martin, an official with San Francisco-based California & Hawaiian Sugar Co., an association of 22 Hawaiian sugar companies that markets all of that state's sugar. C&H refines its sugar in Crockett, Calif., which means raw sugar must be shipped from the islands. "Some of our competitors haven't been affected at all, namely the beet sugar producers" (which produce in the contiguous U.S.), he says.

C&H, which lost about $6 million of business during the strike, plans "to try to recapture the share of the market we had," Mr. Martin says. But he acknowledges some market losses might be permanent.

"There's no question: Some highly-competitive markets (like certain agricultural products) will be lost to foreign competition," says Gordon Larkin, a California state official who has been compiling data on the strike's economic impact.

West Coast longshoremen went on strike July 1 but were ordered back to work Oct. 6 under an 80-day "cooling off" period of a Taft-Hartley injunction. The strike was renewed Jan. 17 after negotiators failed to agree on various issues. Tentative agreement was reached Monday.

While longshoremen are preparing to return to work, businesses are assessing the damage on their profit and loss statements. Mattel Inc., the toy manufacturer, has said it expects to report a loss for the fourth quarter of 1971 partly because of the strike. For the nine months ended Oct. 31, Mattel previously reported a loss of $4 million, as compared with a profit of $14.5 million, or 93 cents a share, a year earlier. Brentwood Industries Inc., Los Angeles, a wig maker whose main plant is in Hong Kong, figures it spent $1 million to import its product during the initial 100 days of the strike—nearly five times what it would ordinarily have cost.

California Valley Exports, the overseas marketing arm for two major producers of canned fruit, estimates sales for the crop year begun July 1, 1971, are running 40% less than a year ago because of the strike. Because California Valley couldn't meet delivery schedules, many customers have turned to other sources, says Percy Rideout, managing director. And there is "no guarantee" the company can win them back, he says.

Even those companies that didn't lose markets as a result of the strike paid dearly to keep them. Robert Freeland, executive vice president of the Rice Growers Association of California, says rice normally is shipped directly from Sacramento to Puerto Rico—the association's major market. But during the strike it was routed by rail to Houston and by ship to Puerto Rico; that proved "very expensive" to the association, which absorbed the extra costs, says Mr. Freeland.

Mazda Motors of America, headquartered near Los Angeles, absorbed about $1.4 million in extra handling charges to bring its cars through alternate ports during the initial 100 days of the strike, reports C. R. Brown, general manager. The strike hit last summer just as the company launched an advertising campaign to introduce its car in California, "but at the time we didn't have enough cars to meet the demand," says Mr. Brown. To make matters worse, a shipload of Mazdas had arrived in port the night before the strike began, and "it took us about eight weeks to get that ship unloaded."

For a few companies, however, the strike was an unexpected bonanza. Flying Tiger Line Inc., the cargo carrier, says its traffic increased substantially as a result of the strike. An official of Seattle-based Airborne Freight Corp., an air freight forwarder, says "we expect to keep" most of the 10% to 15% extra business picked up during the most recent walkout. And the California Beet Grower Association reports that during the strike its 3,000 members have supplied 70% to 75% of all sugar sold in the state, up from a normal 65%. "We've had a windfall from it (the dock strike), there's no question," says Malcolm Young, executive director.

A few companies, like Amfac Inc., a diversified, Honolulu-based concern, figure they can spring back fairly quickly. Amfac figures that its earnings would have been five to seven cents a share higher last year if the dock strike hadn't added to costs. The company reported 1971 earnings of $1.92 a share, up from a restated $1.73 a year earlier. But "there won't be any permanent effect on Amfac" because of the strike, says Henry A. Walker Jr., president. And the national forest products association says the wood-products industry lost about $1 million daily in exports of logs and wood mill residues in Japan, but it expects to recover that market once the strike officially is over.

WHO'S ON FIRST? WHO CARES?

A WALL STREET JOURNAL *News Roundup*

So there's a baseball strike on. So who cares?

Not some of the customers at Zorro's. For the uninitiated, Zorro's is a plush cocktail lounge and restaurant within shouting distance of Anaheim Stadium, home of the California Angels. It's known as a hangout for players and fans alike. But Jody Fox, co-owner of Zorro's, says that so far the fans, at least, are warming up as usual.

In fact, he says, "We have a couple of drunks who are going to the games anyway"—despite the strike and despite the fact that the Angels weren't scheduled to open at home until tomorrow night.

And in Las Vegas, Jimmy the Greek Snyder, who publishes a sports newsletter and lists betting odds, says most bettors and bookmakers he has talked with "don't really care one way or the other about the baseball season's not opening on schedule." However, he has received a few queries from bettors wanting to know what the odds are on having a baseball season at all. But Jimmy the Greek says he isn't quoting odds on that.

In New York, at WOR-TV, which telecasts Met games, Robert L. Glaser, vice president and general manager, says: "I'm particularly surprised at the apathy of the fans. I would have thought we would have found them much more demonstrative."

John Kaleal, however, is demonstrative. "I think it stinks," says a very unapathetic Mr. Kaleal when asked about the players' strike. One reason it "stinks" is that Mr. Kaleal is sales manager of Checker Bar Ice Cream Vending Co. of Cleveland. And his company stands to lose $200 or so every time the Cleveland Indians fail to play a scheduled game at home. Checker Bar vendors probably lose $15 to $20 each per missed game (they split their proceeds about half and half with the company, Mr. Kaleal says). Normally, he adds, there would be about 10 of his vendors selling ice cream, popcorn and peanuts to Cleveland fans.

Pension & Pay

To the clubowners and players, the strike isn't over peanuts, however. The original dispute in the 13-day-old strike—the first in the sport's history—was over pension-fund payments. But when an agreement was reached this week to put $500,000 in surplus earnings from the pension fund into pension benefits, a new dispute cropped up. This revolved around paying the players for the games already missed. As of last night, the issue was unsolved.

Even if many fans are apathetic, the clubowners aren't, for every missed game is costing them money. Some baseball sources say the strike—depending, of course, on its length—may make a difference as to whether some teams make or lose money or break even for the whole year. It is known that only the top three or four finishers in each of the two major leagues generally make a profit each year, and most of their earnings are small.

Some of the games may be made up later, but as one club official puts it, "How can you make up an opening day?" The official is Reuben Askenase, president of Sports Association, which owns the Houston Astros. He says 51,000 fans had been expected to attend the opener with Cincinnati.

Other businesses besides baseball itself are

affected by the walkout—like television and radio, hotels and airlines. But thus far, the damage in general doesn't seem severe.

National Broadcasting Co., for instance, telecasts nationally one or two games each week. The RCA Corp. unit is in the first year of a four-year contract estimated at $70 million to $72 million. One estimate is that the network would be paying about $345,000 for each of the games lost to the strike. But NBC has adopted a "no-play, no-pay" policy.

Ad Revenues

NBC is losing the ad revenue it would have received from each game. It has 20 commercial positions a game, selling for about $20,000 each, or about $400,000 a game. But one ad-agency media man doubts that NBC could sell all spots at the full price at this time of year. "At this point in the season, there are no pennant races and no Vida Blues, and there are playoffs in basketball and hockey. So it's doubtful NBC is really out $400,000."

NBC has turned the time back to its local stations, most of which ran movies last Saturday. WNBC-TV in New York showed "Charge of the Light Brigade" to what it called "very acceptable ratings."

Westinghouse Broadcasting Corp., a unit of Westinghouse Electric Co., owns TV stations in Baltimore, Pittsburgh and Boston that carry the local teams on a regular basis. The strike "has been an inconvenience, but not much more than that," says Chet Collier, the company's TV stations' group president. He adds that "the only way it could hurt us is if the strike were very prolonged and we couldn't make up the games—and the revenues—later on." When a baseball game is canceled, the Westinghouse stations simply pick up a program from the network with which they are affiliated—a profitable practice for the stations.

But one unaffiliated station, WOR in New York, feels that it has been caught off-base by the walkout. Mr. Glaser, the station executive, says the outlet is losing $20,000 for each canceled Mets' game. And as for replacement programming, he says that "WOR is now forced to program on a standby basis, making it very difficult to promote shows on such short notice." WOR is owned by the RKO-General unit of General Tire & Rubber Co.

Some Lose Jobs

Concessionaires, of course, aren't happy about the strike. Illinois Sports Service, Inc., which handles the concessions and programs for the Chicago White Sox, said it has laid off about 300 employes because of the delay in starting the season. The company operates 20 stands in White Sox Park, a spokesman says. He declines to estimate the lost revenue but says sales average about $1 per spectator.

In San Francisco, S. E. Onorato, who operates the Candlestick Park parking lot, figures he lost $15,000 in parking fees for three missed games. "That'll never be made up," he asserts. "Even if those missed games are played as doubleheaders, it'll only attract a handful more people."

Hotels, however, don't seem particularly hard-hit. The Sheraton West Hotel in Los Angeles has agreements with three National League teams that stay there when visiting. The Atlanta Braves had been scheduled to arrive last Monday, but the hotel didn't keep the rooms open for them. At the Jack Tar Hotel, where most teams stay while in San Francisco, the only business lost has been to the San Diego Padres. "We won't be affected until April 24 when the Philadelphia Phillies are scheduled in," says Phil Weiskopf, the general manager. He estimates, however, that if the whole season should be canceled, the hotel would lose $120,000 to $130,000 in revenues.

Airlines in general don't seem to have suffered too much. Ozark Airlines is the official carrier for the new Texas Rangers team of Dallas-Fort Worth—formerly the Washington Senators. A spokesman for the line says the team would normally have chartered several aircraft for out-of-town trips and, as a result, "we've had to fill these aircraft with individual passengers." But, he adds, "It really hasn't been much trouble yet."

Indeed, United Air Lines calls the strike a "kind of blessing in disguise." The subsidiary of UAL Inc. flies 17 of the 24 clubs and hence has lost some charter revenues. But a spokesman says the strike has freed some planes at a time when the carrier needs them because of "high demand" elsewhere.

Some cities as well as businesses stand to lose money. For instance, the city of Anaheim, home of the California Angels, owns the stadium and the grounds. It gets 7½% of the gross admissions, 50% of the parking take and a third of the concessions, says Tom Liegler, stadium and convention-center director. He estimates all that totals $9,000 on an average night.

Meanwhile, back at Zorro's, near the Anaheim Stadium, co-owner Jody Fox is somewhat worried by the strike even if some of his heavier tipplers don't know it's on. For one thing, he fears that business will decline if the strike isn't over by the scheduled opening tomorrow night.

For another, though, his place is a favorite spot of players after the games. "When the players have a night game, it's natural to go out afterward," he says. But with no games scheduled now, he adds, "when the players tell their wives they're going for a workout in the morning, it's tough to explain why they don't get home until 2 a.m."

BIG JOHN'S DILEMMA

By Byron E. Calame
Staff Reporter of The Wall Street Journal

"Big John" Griner, the bulky six-foot president of the American Federation of Government Employes, has laid in a supply of his favorite laryngitis medicine.

He isn't suffering yet. Rather, his secretary explained to Mr. Griner's physician in Washington the other day, he was just stocking up for the biennial convention, opening today in Denver, of the largest union of Federal employes.

"You should come out to the convention," she told the puzzled doctor, "and you'd understand."

He would indeed. Mr. Griner can expect heavy strain on his voice, and on his nerves as well. Militant delegates are preparing to push their moderate chief to be more aggressive in representing them. The convention's actions may renew the threat of strikes against the Government and may bring stiffer pay pressures that could sink Uncle Sam deeper into the red.

A Change in Stance

Though the union's actual membership is just over 300,000, it claims bargaining rights for 600,000 Federal workers, about one-fourth of all those outside the postal service. Its membership is particularly strong in the Labor and Defense Departments, the Social Security Administration and the Veterans Administration.

The no-strike clause in the AFGE constitution is almost certain to be weakened or eliminated at this week's convention. At the last convention, Mr. Griner dramatically defeated a move to delete the clause by threatening to resign if it were passed. Now his stand has changed.

"I've always opposed the right to strike, but we face a situation today where the Government is bringing on itself a case where employes, particularly in the lower (pay) classifications, are going to withhold their services no matter what I try to do," Mr. Griner warned a Congressional subcommittee a few days ago. It was probably the most militant note sounded so far by the Georgian, who has long been known for his low-key, law-abiding approach.

Though the law still bans strikes by Government employes, Mr. Griner's members are mindful that postal workers—who have their own unions—walked out anyway last spring and won plump wage gains. And a group of delegates from over 30 Veterans Administration hospitals is threatening to strike if the convention doesn't act to help them get pay adjustments.

Out of the Denver convention, in any case, will probably come a strong call for full bargaining rights for all Civil Service employes: Their pay rates would be set by negotiation with Government executives rather than through legislation. The postal workers have already won this privilege.

Seeking a Fifth Term

What's more, some union militants have teamed with political enemies of Mr. Griner to mount the most serious effort to defeat him since he was first elected president in 1962. Though the AFGE Committee for Progress in 1970 stands little chance of unseating Mr. Griner in his bid for a fifth two-year term, its campaign is fueling the discontent.

"This convention will make the Democratic convention in Chicago look like a picnic," predicts a Griner backer only half in jest. The union chief himself concedes the mood of the delegates isn't going to be mellowed by Congressional passage last week of legislation giving mailmen an 8% raise that won't go to other Federal workers.

Ever since last spring's postal strike, Mr. Griner has been getting more and more heat from his membership. He calls rank-and-file unrest his "major problem" these days. Half of the 63-year-old AFGE leader's travels since the mailmen's walkout, aides estimate, have been required to cool down "uprisings by militants" in the union. Among the loudest complaints: Pay in the Government trails pay in private employment, and Uncle Sam is moving too slowly toward the Federal goal of "comparability" with industry.

If the union's militants ever work themselves up to the point of striking, the effect would, of course, be felt most keenly in those agencies—Labor, Defense and the Social Security and Veterans Administrations—where the AFGE is strongest. But Mr. Griner doubts that a strike by his members could ever be effective, simply because they aren't concentrated in vital facilities as the postmen are.

Bold Defiance of Law

The willingness of some other public-employe union leaders to resort to strikes points up the contrast between them and Mr. Griner. Members of the State, County and Municipal Employes Union and the American Federation of Teachers as well as the postal unions have boldly struck in defiance of law; they have often managed to win attractive pay increases with a minimum of punishment. Yet Mr. Griner has clung to the traditional Federal employe union techniques of lobbying and cajoling on Capitol Hill and in the Executive Branch.

Now even AFGE officers friendly to Mr. Griner feel a change is due.

"Our sister unions have far outstripped us," frets Joseph Gleason, an AFGE national vice president and a long-time Griner backer. "Our entire set of attitudes—especially the good-guys routine at the table of Congress—has to be changed," he declares. An officer of a Veterans Administration local, who also supports the union chief, warns that "if he (Griner) isn't a little more militant, we'll have to do something ourselves."

Among the union's rebels, Farrel Vincent, chairman of the Committee for Progress and president of a Tennessee local, says, "Griner's made a great contribution, but the times have passed him by." Mr. Vincent claims "some locals will stop paying dues unless the leadership becomes more militant; they're no longer con-

tent to pay dues into a social club."

In Oklahoma, a spokesman for a group of dissidents in AFGE Local 916 at Tinker Air Force Base claims that the unit's membership has declined to 7,100 from nearly 9,000 less than five years ago because of the "indifferent attitude" of Mr. Griner and other union officials. The insurgent predicts that the local will lose another 2,000 members by September if "changes (in leadership) are not made nationally as well as locally."

Mr. Griner, who's acknowledged a hard worker (14 hours a day and 200,000 miles of traveling a year) even by many of his critics, replies in his calm drawl: "We're molding this federation into more of a union. It's gradual, but we had a long way to go." Tom Smith, a candidate for national secretary-treasurer and a Griner supporter, agrees: "Six years ago, we were 50 years behind the rest of the labor movement; today, we're only 25 years behind. We've come a long way."

Indeed, the union's membership under Mr. Griner has soared to about 315,000 today from only 106,000 in 1962. (Its nearest rival, the National Association of Government Employes, is less than one-third as big.) Because it also holds bargaining rights for many nonmembers, it now claims to represent more than a quarter of the 2.2 million Civil Service workers, though the last official tally made last November showed less.

Mr. Griner has come a long way, too. After graduating from the Camilla, Ga., high school in 1924, he worked for various railroads for 11 years. He went to work for the Government's Railroad Retirement Board in 1936, eventually becoming a labor relations officer in 1951. He had gotten a law degree in 1940 and been elected a national vice president of AFGE in 1946. He moved up to the AFGE presidency in 1962 and last fall won election to the policy-making executive council of the AFL-CIO.

The seat on the council may help Mr. Griner lead the way to AFL-CIO President George Meany's goal of "a new day in Federal employer-employe relationships." In any case, it has made Mr. Griner's handling of this week's convention of greater-than-usual interest to the labor movement. "The AFGE could become one of the most important unions in the country," says an official of a large AFL-CIO affiliate, "but I have a great feeling that Griner can't cut the mustard."

Convention consideration of the no-strike clause is expected to stir the most debate. Mr. Griner, squinting as he's prone to do when tackling a ticklish point, concedes his position has changed. He says he won't fight a modification that might make the AFGE constitution say only that "this organization is opposed to strikes or picketing." The present clause states that "AFGE is opposed to and will not engage in strikes."

Daniel Kearney, an AFGE vice president who is the Committee for Progress' presidential candidate, promises that the insurgents, if elected, "would press for the right to strike in certain instances." He explains: "Some services aren't so essential. In those situations, we should have the opportunity to seek redress of our grievances by striking."

A Law-Abiding Citizen

Mr. Gleason, who's backing Mr. Griner for the presidency, wants the no-strike clause removed, too. "If our people are ever compelled to do it (strike)," he argues, "at least their own union shouldn't have to punish them." Another reason for his position: A recent straw poll taken by a local in New York and New Jersey showed over 80% of those responding would support a move to call in sick at the same time for at least two days' duration.

Mr. Griner, however, contends that no more than 15% of AFGE's members would go on strike if a walkout were ever called. "It would take 90% or more to make a strike work," he figures. And in a voice quavering slightly with emotion, he declares:

"The law says you can't strike. As an individual, I'm a law-abiding citizen and the great majority of the membership is. We're bound by the law."

But Tom Smith, who heads the AFGE's largest local, a 14,000-member unit at the Social Security headquarters in Baltimore, contends Mr. Griner is likely to change his views eventually. Mr. Smith's reasoning: "John Griner is going to follow his people's feelings. So when everyone decides to go (on strike), he would support it; he'd have to."

Some delegates to this week's convention appear ready to force the strike issue. Mrs. Ruth Beecher, secretary-treasurer of a VA hospital local in Batavia, N.Y., warns that the militant VA hospital delegates, representing over 80 locals from 14 states, are "willing to do anything necessary" to get action on their demands for a revamping of the VA's procedures for classifying jobs; the group claims many of its members are paid less than employes in comparable jobs in other agencies.

Open Threats of Strike

Mr. Griner says he's been promised "relief" for the hospital workers. But Mrs. Beecher warns that "the members of our group are determined to get some kind of specific action taken by the convention. If something isn't done, all hell is going to break loose." Others talk openly of the possibility of a strike.

The gains won by the postal workers in their first bargaining over pay are expected to spark substantial support among the delegates for applying the concept for other Government workers. The AFL-CIO has said it will propose such a bill shortly.

Until recently Mr. Griner had shown little enthusiasm for the idea. "It's coming," he now declares. "It's right upon us." Still, he suggests that it will be "a long time" before he will be ready to "rely on (negotiated) contracts completely."

The present arrangement that lets Federal employe unions negotiate only such matters as working conditions, grievance procedures and promotion policies, and not on pay, is one the AFGE president has apparently mastered. The union's growth has been aided greatly by his skillful lobbying in Congress, at the Civil Service Commission and with the bureaucrats who are his members' bosses.

Last year he was able to block a pay bill that would have given postal workers a raise almost double that slated for all other Federal employes. And during the postal bargaining last spring, he wangled a promise from key legislators that the initial 6% wage boost won by the mailmen would also go to all white-collar employes. But he hasn't been able to fulfill his April promise that AFGE would win Congressional approval by July 1 of pay raises averaging at least 10% for all Federal workers and a $6,000 minimum-annual salary.

One of AFGE's best friends on Capitol Hill until his defeat in 1968 was Sen. Mike Monroney, Oklahoma Democrat. "John Griner has a real good grasp of things," Mr. Monroney says. "He's reasonable and appreciative. He's forceful, but not an antagonizing person. He boils over, cools down, and then boils over again until he's got all he can."

Mr. Griner's secret at the Civil Service Commission, a top official confides, is that "he inches his way to a lot of progress." The official continues: "He rants and raves and gets very emotional. Yet he always makes clear that his demands are negotiable. And he's usually ready to settle for 50% of what he's asking for."

Providing Help and Advice

A mainspring in the AFGE's growth, according to Mr. Griner, has been his emphasis on providing help and advice to members who were confused or abused by the Government's personnel regulations. Since he became president, the number of full-time AFGE field representatives has been increased to 120 from a tiny 13. An education program has taught hundreds of local officials how to better unravel personnel red tape and handle grievances for their members.

The rapid membership growth since 1962 has provided the wherewithal for the expanded field staff and education programs. The annual budget has climbed to $4.8 million from only $955,000 eight years ago.

But now, Mr. Griner concedes, the union's growth rate has slowed sharply. He estimates the union is showing a net gain of about 1,000 members a month. "Back in 1966," recalls an AFGE staffer, "we were picking up recruits like crazy—often 5,000 members a month."

One reason for the slowdown is that layoffs, especially in the Defense Department, have drained away some members. But another aspect of the slowdown raises a fundamental question about future growth.

Much of AFGE's rapid expansion during the 1960s came among Federal blue-collar workers, many of whom had union backgrounds; now the AFGE recruiters are turning more toward Uncle Sam's white-collar employes, and Mr. Griner admits the going is tougher. Only 29% of them are organized thus far.

'BEST OFFER' ARBITRATION'S CRITICS

By Byron E. Calame

WASHINGTON — President Nixon calls it the "Crippling Strikes Prevention Act," and on paper it looks seductively simple.

The idea is to avert disruptive strikes against railroads and other transportation industries, and the heart of the Nixon proposal is the "final offer selection" procedure. In theory, it would work something like this:

Suppose union-management negotiations have deadlocked, with the union demanding a 12% raise and management offering 8%. A strike looms. Instead, the President orders each side to submit its "last best offer" to an impartial panel. The union comes down to 11% and management comes up to 9%. The panel then picks one offer or the other—it doesn't have the authority to split the difference—and imposes it. That's all there's to it: The bargaining is over, the strike averted.

Backers of the administration plan, now bogged down on Capitol Hill, see it as a real advance over existing procedures. They contend it would force bargainers for both sides to narrow their differences; each would be trying to persuade the panel that its position was the more reasonable one. Supporters argue that this is a big improvement over compulsory arbitration, which offers greater latitudes to the arbitrators and tends to encourage negotiators to stake out extreme positions in the expectation that arbitrators will split the difference. Indeed, some high administration officials insist that if Congress would only pass their bill, nationally crippling transportation strikes would be a thing of the past.

Questions of Workability

But critics of the administration's proposal are raising serious questions about its workability, questions that Senate opponents of the plan are citing in fighting the measure. And most of the labor relations arbitrators, mediators and professors who have publicly expressed their views of the new procedure say it wouldn't avert all emergency transportation strikes.

Are the arbitrators and mediators against the plan because it would cut them out of their jobs? This is the argument of administration officials. Yet it would seem that while their roles might be diminished in time by the new procedure, experienced arbitrators would always be required to help man the selection panels the procedure would require—and, of course, to handle the great bulk of labor disputes that don't create any "national emergency."

Essentially, the critics doubt the Nixon plan would be flexible enough to allow the trade-offs and compromises that are so much a part of the bargaining process. They fear that the impartial panels would often find themselves choosing the "least unreasonable" of two rival offers. Further, the winner-take-all nature of the process could make it hard for union leaders to keep their rank-and-filers in line in cases where the employer's offer is selected, they say.

Top administration officials who developed the idea insist they're not dissuaded by this litany of infirmities. Their reasoning: In the overall perspective, the proposal's unpalatableness may well be its key strength. The prime argument for the measure, one of its principal architects suggests, is that the parties, in effect, would be so fearful of resorting to the final offer option that they would reach agreement voluntarily. The fact that the procedure could prove unfair to one side "constitutes a strong disincentive to use it," asserts Undersecretary of Labor Laurence Silberman.

Organized labor opposes the Nixon plan as being nothing more than sugar-coated compulsory arbitration, and President Nixon himself acknowledged as much during his recent visit to John Connally's ranch in Texas. Whatever else that one can say about compulsory arbitration, it hasn't proved itself to be a panacea for averting strikes.

A study of Australia's compulsory arbitration system published in a recent issue of the Labor Department's Monthly Labor Review makes this point. Under the system, working days lost as a result of strikes spurted to 3.1 million last year from 2.4 million in 1970 and only 1.1 million in 1968, according to the analysis, which was written by Kingsley Laffer, associate professor of industrial relations at the University of Sidney.

With the administration hoping for a Senate vote this year on the measure, the White House appears to be gearing up to take its case to the public again just as it did during the recent West Coast dock tieup. One reason: Public sentiment stirred up by the administration during the West Coast walkout spurred a test vote in the Senate on the legislation—and the measure lost by a surprisingly close 42 to 39 margin.

Shortly after asking Congress last February to pass stopgap legislation to resolve the dock strike, Mr. Nixon contended in a special message to Congress that the walkout could have been averted by the enactment of his permanent reform. The message was intended "to emphasize again to the Congress and to the American people" that Mr. Nixon's broad reform would have made it "unnecessary to come up (to Congress) with this request for *ad hoc* legislation," a high administration official explained at a White House briefing.

An 'Arsenal' of Weapons

Mr. Nixon's proposal would supposedly give him an "arsenal" of three weapons for settling emergency disputes in the rail, trucking, airline, longshore and maritime industries. In addition to invoking the final-offer procedure, he could require partial operation of the affected industry (anathema to management) or order an extension of no-strike periods provided for in existing laws. The theory: If the parties aren't sure which wea-

pon the President will fire at them first in a strike, the uncertainty will spur them to reach a voluntary agreement.

Nevertheless, the final offer option is the "guts" of the bill and the alternative the President would use most of the time, almost everyone agrees. Specifically, it would require each side to submit either one or two "final offers" for consideration by a neutral three-member· panel: Each offer would have to "constitute a complete bargaining agreement and resolve all the issues involved in the dispute."

The question, of course, is whether the procedure will work. That question obviously can't be answered with certainty. The procedure has not been tested so the sharply-differing opinions about it are based largely on conjecture. But several veteran arbitrators and mediators have seriously questioned the workability of the procedure in testimony and statements being gathered by congressional committees.

The final offer approach "isn't a panacea," asserts William Simkin, former head of the Federal Mediation and Conciliation Service under Presidents Kennedy and Johnson. "I would suggest, of the cases with which I have been intimately familiar, that (in) only a fraction—substantially less than half— would this have been feasible," he told a Senate subcommittee recently. Even some administration labor relations experts concede they respect Mr. Simkin's views.

The Nixon proposal "assumes that on all issues in bargaining there is a middle ground," frets Theodore Kheel, veteran New York arbitrator and mediator. "Perhaps the wage issue can be put in this category. But not the most difficult (issue) of labor relations in recent years: the elimination of jobs as the result of technological change. . . . This issue is never a simple clash of two opposing views which can be decided on an either-or basis."

Manning and work rule issues "require delicate neutral adjustment between valid but conflicting positions," writes Charles Rehmus, co-director of the Institute of Labor and Industrial Relations run by the University of Michigan and Wayne State University. "Final-offer arbitration does not permit this process to operate where it is most needed," he asserts, citing three public-sector disputes where the procedure was tried.

Mr. Rehmus reports that the procedure failed in disputes in Massachusetts and Michigan where the labor issues involved work

rules. "The parties remained poles apart, and
the neutrals refused to select any of the offers
because all were deemed unreasonable," he
explains. (The Nixon plan would force the
panel to make a choice.) In a New York dispute where the sole issue was pay, however,
the final-offer approach proved effective because "dollar differences are almost infinitely
divisible," he observes.

Since the panel can't modify the offers, it
might have to accept certain inequities in
making a choice, some labor relations experts
fear. Mediator David Cole, "a highly regarded old pro" in the words of Labor Secretary James Hodgson, recently outlined how
such a dilemma might develop where the final-offer procedure is used:

Mr. Cole suggested union bargainers might
decide "we will make a more modest (wage)
request than we have been holding out for,
but we will put in all these work rules and
things we like. The board . . . will like our
money offer—they will think we are modest
about that. So they will accept ours, and, boy,
we will have a contract that will really do the
job for us.

"Or, vice-versa, the employer may make
something that looks like a generous wage
offer, (but) put in a lot of working conditions
the union cannot live with. But the board cannot separate them out—they have got to give
the union the whole works."

The win-lose atmosphere of the final offer
scheme troubles some labor-relations men.
"The package selected . . . will be an imposed settlement that will represent a victory
for one side and a defeat for the other," cautions W. Glen Harlan, Eastern Airlines' senior
vice president for legal affairs, in a recent
American Bar Association Journal article.
Merton Bernstein, Ohio State University law
professor, takes the problem a step further:
"Anyone with labor-relations experience
knows that whenever a winner and a loser
may be identified, the leadership of the loser
is likely, if only to regain face, to cause
trouble."

While Messrs. Simkin, Cole and Kheel, all
practicing arbitrators, have showed up to
publicly question the final offer process during recent Senate hearings on the Nixon bill,
only one specialist testified in favor of the
measure. Other specialists have filed statements backing and opposing the bill. Almost
every specialist stating an opinion, however,
concedes the final offer procedure won't prevent all emergency transportation strikes.

Bernard Meltzer, a well-known arbitrator
and law professor at the University of Chicago, maintains that the final-offer option
would "stimulate both parties to engage in
reasonable and responsible negotiations."
While rating the process an improvement over
the present mediation procedures, he admits
"there are naturally some circumstances in
which its availability might not produce the
expected results in bargaining or in which its
use might involve special difficulties."

The Labor Department recently issued a
press release summarizing the opinions of
several professors who have filed statements
favoring the bill. But the professors and the
parties on the firing line don't always agree.
Eaton Conant, director of the University of
Oregon's Institute of Industrial and Labor Relations, reported "limited experience" with a
final-offer option plan in the city of Eugene,
Ore., "indicates it can work."

A city official interviewed concedes that
Eugene's first use of the procedure did force
a settlement in a March dispute with firemen,
but he notes that there are growing signs that
the terms of the imposed pact won't be fully
honored by the disgruntled union members. A
union leader agrees that some "harassment"
by resentful firemen is already occurring.
Thus, the city official concludes flatly: "It's
not working." Both union and city officials
confess they were surprised when the three-
member panel picked the lower of the city's
two alternative final offers by a two-to-one
vote; the city's offers were 6% and 6.5%, the
union's final demands were 7.5% and 8.8%,
according to the municipal official.

Several professors agree with Donald Cullen of Cornell's School of Industrial and Labor
Relations, who has testified that he would like
to see the "challenging new idea" tried. Harvard economics professor Carl Stevens concedes that "some of the answers to questions
about its workability can only be had by actual trial." Mr. Cullen figures that "if by
some quirk a truly disastrous contract did result in some case, Congress could presumably
undo the damage by passing a law that would
set aside that particular award."

All Imperfect, So . . .

Almost everyone who has analyzed the
Nixon administration proposal can probably
agree with Mr. Meltzer that "all procedures
for dealing with critical transportation strikes
are likely to be imperfect." So it might be
worthwhile sticking with the often untidy mediation procedures that now exist for a while
longer—and for several reasons.

There are some indications that selective strikes—or lockouts—could be used more to create the pressure needed to produce voluntary settlements. The most recent major labor dispute on the railroads was voluntarily settled last August after an 18-day selective strike against 10 carriers by the United Transportation Union. And major maritime unions have recently pledged to work with management to try to voluntarily set up machinery that would lead to the binding arbitration of disputes.

Moreover, it appears that many of the transportation walkouts that were labeled "national emergencies" weren't really that damaging. Despite some White House efforts to downgrade its conclusions, no one has ever really refuted a study prepared in 1969 at the direction of then Labor Secretary Shultz. It determined that three Atlantic and Gulf Coast Longshoremen's strikes between 1962 and 1969 had a "minimal" impact on the national economy. Earlier this year, the Pay Board's staff concluded that the strike by West Coast dockers didn't create a national crisis either.

None of this adds up to what the administration is claiming for its plan: a sweeping, guaranteed solution to the problem of emergency strikes in the transportation industry. Other efforts to improve the present collective bargaining system are cautious and sometimes painful steps forward, not the kind of fundamental breakthroughs the administration is promising.

But the evidence indicates that the administration may well be overselling its solution. The arbitrators, mediators and academic experts closest to the problem generally agree that, at best, the administration proposal would not solve all crippling transportation labor disputes. At worst, it could often prove unworkable. Over the long haul, the continuing search for a better way to resolve emergency disputes may be hindered if the White House raises false hopes now.

AN END TO BARGAINING CLIFF-HANGERS?

By JACK H. MORRIS

PITTSBURGH—Is the pendulum of collective bargaining swinging away from an era of confrontation to one of accommodation?

The startling news from the labor front in recent weeks certainly gives that impression. The strike-prone Railroad Brotherhoods, for the first time in their history, have agreed to a new wage and benefits package in advance of their contract deadline. More importantly, the powerful United Steelworkers of America reached an accord with the 10 largest steelmakers to avoid their usual cliff-hanging negotiations when their contract expires next year by taking a no-strike pledge and promising to submit unresolved issues to binding arbitration.

The prospect that the steel settlement might be the model for other major labor contracts "is breathtaking," editorialized the Pittsburgh Post-Gazette. Across the country other newspapers and officials high up in the Nixon administration echoed that viewpoint as the President last week named a blue ribbon panel to explore strike alternatives in other industries. Called the National Commission for Industrial Peace, the 11-member body pointedly includes both I. W. Abel, president of the Steelworkers, and R. Heath Larry, vice chairman of U.S. Steel Corp. and the steel industry's top negotiator.

A Difficult Path

"There's a great groping for a strikeless society," notes Robert Coulson, president of the American Arbitration Association. Nevertheless, those most familiar with the steel agreement and those who have explored its application elsewhere fear that few unions will be able to comfortably follow in the Steel-workers' footsteps. The path is likely to be particularly difficult for those unions whose strikes cause the greatest public pain and provoke the loudest outcry for a remedy—unions in such vital public services as transportation, police and fire protection, education, health and sanitation.

"I hope the President's committee doesn't become like the War on Poverty and promise more than it can deliver," says Mr. Larry.

A pragmatic executive, Mr. Larry is troubled that people like AFL-CIO President George Meany and Commerce Secretary Dent ascribe such words as "labor-management statesmanship" to an agreement that took him and Mr. Abel the better part of five years to work out. "I don't understand statesmanship," Mr. Larry says. "Most people act out of self interest. The best we can look for [in bringing about labor peace] is for true enlightened self interest to come into play."

Self interest—perhaps self preservation—was certainly the motivating factor in steel's bargaining breakthrough. No industry has been so ravished by the boom-bust cycle of its triennial labor negotiations as has steel. Although there hasn't been a steel strike in 14 years, contracts, which are negotiated on an industry-wide basis, invariably are settled on the very brink of a nationwide walkout. Uncertain of uninterrupted supplies, major steel users begin scrambling months in advance of contract negotiations to hoard away the metal. Steel mills are forced into costly overtime to meet the demand and foreign producers fill their order books for long-term commitments.

Then when a contract is concluded, buyers live off their stockpiles and import purchases, mills bank their furnaces and count their losses and steelworkers are placed on extensive layoffs. Hedge buying cost the 10 largest steelmakers an estimated $80 million when the last contract was signed in 1971, and the process put 100,000 steelworkers out of work, some of whom have never been recalled.

By eliminating even the threat of a strike well in advance of their August 1974 contract deadline, industry and labor leaders hope they have ended the need for hedge buying and have dealt imports a serious blow as well.

But the agreement, while unprecedented, is also experimental. Both Mr. Abel and Mr. Larry acknowledge that the pact may not be extended beyond 1977 if either party feels burned in the negotiations—and/or arbitration—on specific issues which must yet take place. Students of collective bargaining consider it unlikely that other major unions will want to surrender their ultimate weapon—the strike—until they see how well it works in steel. Furthermore, few other industries have the ingredients for a similar settlement: industrywide bargaining in a key area of the economy, costly stockpiling, painful post-agreement layoffs and rising imports.

The presidents of two of the largest unions with contracts expiring this year—Leonard Woodcock of the United Auto Workers and Peter Bommarito of the United Rubber Workers—have flatly rejected the steel approach in their bargaining. Both unions direct their strike threat against a target company, not the industry, and thus a strike wouldn't inflict the same wounds on the economy. Besides, without the inducement of stockpile-caused layoffs, "our members wouldn't go for arbitration," adds Mr. Bommarito. The Teamsters, whose national contract expires June 30, prefer local or regional strikes to national ones and thus aren't looking to steel for a model settlement, a spokesman says.

Aluminum, Electrics and Imports

Can companies and aluminum makers bargain on an industry-wide basis, but cans are too bulky to easily stockpile and with many independent and non-unionized aluminum producers, there's not much need for it in that industry. Contracts in the electrical industry, where major negotiations are currently underway, involve so many unions with different expiration dates—45 in the case of Westinghouse—that a unified approach like steel's is impossible.

Even some industries with import problems find little inducement to follow the Steelworkers' lead. Merchants don't stockpile dresses or buy foreign labels when a contract with the International Ladies' Garment Workers is about to expire. "People wouldn't stockpile steel either if it had a hemline," an ILGW spokesman says. Although 25% of the ladieswear sold in this country is imported, "The fulcrum for moving these imports isn't a change in collective bargaining, but a change in legislation in Washington," the spokesman adds.

And, since police protection and garbage collection can't be stockpiled in advance, there's little parallel between nationwide bargaining in heavy industry and the fragmented bargaining of municipal workers employed by 25,000 local governmental agencies.

There are reasons other than economics, of course, why a new negotiating stance came first in steel. "A pact like this requires a solidly entrenched leadership and you don't find Abel's strength in many unions," notes Jack Stieber, director of Michigan State's School of Labor and Industrial Relations. Mr. Abel was reelected without opposition earlier this year to a third and final four-year term as president of the 1.4 million member union. He has the solid backing of his 28-member executive board, and he is currently considered a likely candidate to succeed Mr. Meany someday as head of the AFL-CIO.

In addition, Mr. Abel has achieved substantial gains for his membership through arbitration in the past, particularly in 1968 when he decided to submit to binding arbitration the politically touchy issue of incentive pay. "The USW happens to be far more sophisticated in labor relations than any union I've encountered in 30 years of labor law practice," one professional arbitrator says. "It takes guts and sophistication and experience to come up with an innovative plan like this. Those aren't things that can be transferred to another union."

A joint union-management effort to win rank and file support for a "better way to bargain" in the steel industry had been underway for months despite the fact that worker ratification of a new contract wasn't necessary. A movie, "Where's Joe?" depicting jobs lost to imported steel during contract negotiations had been shown on local television in many steeltowns, bringing the message into the workers' homes. Thus there was little opposition when Mr. Abel dropped his bargaining bombshell at a specially called meeting of 600 local union leaders who form his basic steel industry conference. The new pact was approved by voice vote.

A major deterrent for unions like the Auto Workers and Machinists to follow the steel pact is that they couldn't give up their right to strike without rank-and-file ratification. Under Tony Boyle, the United Mine Workers, who shut down the nation's coalfields for seven weeks in 1971, didn't require rank-and-file approval on their contracts. But Mr. Boyle was ousted last year and insurgent President Arnold Miller vows that next year's settlement will be submitted to a vote of his membership. "I wouldn't anticipate us signing any no-strike clause so long as miners get no sick pay and only get two weeks vacation after 10 years of work," a UMW spokesman says. "We've got a lot of catching up to do before we can consider arbitration."

It's possible, of course, that the steel pact "may have some psychological impact in other areas where there's a need to find a better way to bargain," says Elliott Bredhoff, a Washington labor lawyer and special counsel to the USW. Now that Mr. Abel has demonstrated the courage to accept arbitration, perhaps unions in other industries with different sets of problems can risk experimenting, too.

There are few examples in American labor history where contract arbitration has been freely agreed to by both parties in advance of negotiation. (Grievance arbitration, on the other hand, is widely accepted.) In wage bargaining, arbitration is usually a last ditch ploy invoked only when an impasse has been reached and a strike is imminent. Frequently, it's sought only by the weaker party at the bargaining table, which may explain why the Seafarers and other maritime unions are the only ones considered likely to follow the steel model anytime soon. The maritime unions in the past have rarely reached an agreement until after the President has invoked the Taft-Hartley Act, imposing a 90-day cooling off period.

In some cases, arbitration is little more than a gimmick employed by one side seeking an advantage in bargaining. The Amalgamated Transit Union, which represents bus drivers and a few remaining streetcar operators, for years has required that a local union must submit its case to arbitration before a strike can be called. This hasn't prevented strikes in the industry, but when they do occur, it's put the onus on the employers who have refused to arbitrate.

Somewhat surprisingly, in the case of teachers and municipal workers, where strikes provoke the loudest public outcry, it's often the employer and not the union that refuses arbitration. Last November, the National League of Cities adopted a resolution opposing arbitration on the ground that it usurped the political power of mayors and councilmen. Arbitrators, they fear, might award big pay increases which would necessitate politically unpopular tax increases. During the recent 54-day teachers' strike in Philadelphia, the Board of Education at first rejected a union offer of arbitration on the ground that the board lacked independent taxing authority and thus couldn't guarantee they'd have the funds to meet an arbitrator's settlement. Later, after a state-appointed fact finder issued a report favorable to the board, the tables were turned. The board offered to arbitrate, but the teachers refused.

Compulsory Arbitration Disliked

Seven states have compulsory arbitration for police and firemen, but neither municipal nor union officials seem pleased with the results. Without the danger of stockpiling and layoffs, about the only inducement municipalities and their employes have for voluntary arbitration is the threat that the state legislature or the courts will impose compulsory arbitration on them. Indeed, it was the threat of national legislation to end transportation strikes that pushed the Railroad Brotherhoods toward an early settlement of their contract last month.

It's unlikely that the President's Commission for Industrial Peace will prescribe arbitration unless it can be made palatable to both sides. "I'm very nervous about impressing arbitration on any industry," says Mr. Larry, the U.S. Steel executive. Both he and Mr. Abel have expressed the hope that they will be able to negotiate the remaining terms of their contract without calling in a third party. "If we must go to arbitration, I'll regard it as a point of failure," Mr. Larry says. "Arbitration wasn't put in our agreement to be used. It simply gives us a terminal point to negotiations other than a strike."

The most important element in the new steel pact, says Mr. Stieber of Michigan State, is that "the parties have already agreed on some significant issues in advance, so there's not that much negotiating yet to be done." The three-year pact guarantees a minimum 3% yearly wage increase and cost of living benefits, plus a novel $150 bonus to be paid to each worker when the contract goes into effect in 1974.

Perhaps James Bird, a steel specialist with W. E. Hutton & Co. in New York, has discovered the key to labor peace when he calls the bonus "a fantastic way to buy off a strike."

DEFIANCE OF EVERYTHING

By William D. Hartley
Staff Reporter of The Wall Street Journal

MELBOURNE, Australia — Clever school-children everywhere know about that handy pouch that Australian animals have for carrying their young: the marsupium. And smart negotiators everywhere know about that convenient device the Australian government has for settling the nation's labor-management disputes: arbitration.

For almost 70 years, whenever labor and management have been unable to agree, they have volunteered to take their arguments before the Conciliation and Arbitration Commission. The panel first attempts to coax the parties to an agreement and, if that fails, it then sets the terms of a settlement.

As a result, Australia is often looked to for guidance by frustrated negotiators in the U.S., Canada and Britain who are fed up with the failure of bargaining to prevent long and expensive strikes. Arbitration, it often seems, is an attractive alternative way to reach speedy and reasonable solutions without debilitating shutdowns and a particularly appropriate way to deal with strikes by public-service employes, such as policemen, firemen and teachers.

But if outsiders look at the Australian system carefully, what they see these days is a system that is unraveling.

Banking Disruption

Last December, when government arbitrators cut in half a wage demand by the nation's bank clerks, thousands of them refused to handle checks for several days, thus paralyzing the banking system.

In Sydney, government arbitrators rejected a labor demand for a second man to help the driver operate double-decker buses. In protest the drivers struck for three weeks.

It is true, however, that the great majority of the 3,000 cases that are brought before the federal commission every year are still settled amicably. And strikes are still rare enough to command a prominence in newspapers—an attention that perhaps exaggerates their importance. Still, confidence in arbitration—or at least in the mechanics of the present system— is dwindling, not only among employers and workers but among government officials as well.

The arbitration system was enacted in 1904 in the aftermath of agonizing years of strife between workers and employers. Basically the system works like this: The law created the Conciliation and Arbitration Commission, which consists of "not less than" nine members; the number has varied through the years. The panel is appointed by the federal government.

When a dispute occurs, the employer involved may notify the commission, which appoints a conciliator. If the conciliator can't get the two sides to reach an agreement, he becomes an arbitrator, who decrees a settlement. If the union fails to accept his terms and walks out, the employer goes to the Industrial Court and asks for a strike ban. The court was created by the same 1904 law as the commission but is a separate body. If the union ignores the ban and a subsequent injunction, it is fined. (Thus far, management has never refused to accept the arbitrator's settlement.)

Now, however, some unions are refusing to pay the fines, and in some instances they appear to be receiving a measure of public support.

Clarence O'Shea, a streetcar-union official, refused to pay a $9,700 fine and was sent to jail, but an advertising man dug into his lottery winnings and paid Mr. O'Shea's fine. In another case, a Methodist minister came up with $5,000 to pay the fines of seven unions. The money, he said, came from a business organization (which apparently shelled out to keep the peace).

What has gone wrong?

"It isn't a weakness in the system," one businessman insists. "It wouldn't matter what system we had—we'd have open defiance of it. We're going through the Harry Bridges stage —defiance of everything."

A Change of Mood

Certainly the mood of Australia's 2.5 million union members is far more aggressive now than it was in the 1930s, when workers were grateful just to be employed. Rising prosperity since World War II and almost full employment have emboldened labor and made unions more sure of themselves and more assertive of their socialist ideology.

"The older labor leaders had the attitude of not doing anything that might threaten jobs," one senior government official says. "Today's labor leaders are those who have known little but the affluent society. They feel that they have a weapon in the strike. They don't lose anything that they can't make up in another job."

The archetype of the new labor leader is 40-year-old Robert Hawke, the erudite president of the Australian Council of Trade Unions, roughly the Australian equivalent of the AFL-CIO. From the ACTU's headquarters here, Mr. Hawke, a Rhodes scholar, directs the 1.7 million-member organization with an eloquent authority previously unknown in the blue-collar Australian labor movement.

The Labor View

His critics, not surprisingly, consider Mr. Hawke arrogant and argumentative. This opinion is bolstered somewhat by Mr. Hawke's television appearances, during which he comes across as something of a William Buckley Jr. —only on the other end of the ideological spectrum and without Mr. Buckley's compensating humor. Union members, however, treat him with a respect that sometimes approaches reverence and that has given rise to such popular quips as: "Did you hear what happened to Bob Hawke? He was knocked down by the Sydney Harbor Ferry while walking to work."

From Mr. Hawke's point of view, defiance of the arbitration system or at least of the fines is neither arrogance nor recalcitrance but simply an attempt to right a balance that has long been tipped in favor of management. Why should unions have to pay fines for striking, Mr. Hawke and other labor leaders ask, when employers don't have to pay fines for price-fixing? Most observers agree that Mr. Hawke's point on price-fixing is well-taken and that management is hardly blameless for the malaise that affects labor relations.

Regardless of where the fault lies, there is no question that strikes are on the rise. "We are in the most difficult labor period since the end of World War II," says a government official handling labor questions. Last year about three million working days were lost because of stoppages; four years earlier it was 705,000.

To try to halt the trend, the government has proposed changes in the law, but elections will probably be held next fall or winter, and the whole problem is likely to become entangled in politics.

Under the government proposal, the penalties would be retained, but the conciliator and the arbitrator wouldn't be the same person. Both labor and management say they have given confidential information to the conciliator only to have him use it publicly when he becomes the arbitrator.

The final resolution of the dilemma may well lie outside the arbitration system. In some industries where there have been powerful unions, such as airlines, oil, pulp and paper, there is a long history of collective bargaining. And as unions continue to merge and grow stronger, the trend toward collective bargaining is expected to continue. With some irony, then, as other countries look to Australia for guidance, the Australians themselves are looking elsewhere for models. "Within the process of conciliation," Ian McFee, director of the Victoria Chamber of Commerce believes, "we will arrive at something similar to U.S. collective bargaining."

ON THE LINE - I

By WALTER MOSSBERG
Staff Reporter of THE WALL STREET JOURNAL

WIXOM, Mich.—The woman on the assembly line at the big Ford Motor Co. plant here was upset. The spray gun she was using was leaking all over her work apron, and the sealant solution squirting out of the nozzle was too thin and runny. She had complained to her foreman, but nothing had been done.

Then Charlie Bragg came strolling down the line, and things began to happen. After Mr. Bragg was apprised of the woman's problem, he had a conference with the foreman. Then he called the department responsible for fixing tools. In short order, the woman had a new nozzle and a new barrel of sealant.

Problems brought to Charlie Bragg's attention aren't always dispatched quite so expeditiously. Nevertheless few fault him for lack of initiative. He might be called, in fact, "the fixer"—the man to whom workers can turn in times of trouble. For Mr. Bragg is the union committeeman in the plant's Thunderbird trim-department, and he comes to the people on the line because they can't come to him.

Officially, the 37-year-old Mr. Bragg is a "district committeeman," a local official of the United Auto Workers Union, elected by the 287 people in his department to serve as the full-time representative with management. (The company pays his salary.) But unofficially, Mr. Bragg *is* the union to his people. He is the first and often the only union representative they deal with, and he is every bit as important to them as is Leonard Woodcock, the UAW president, who is leading the union in its current contract talks with Ford.

As one of the several thousand district committeemen in the nation's 44 auto assembly plants, Charlie Bragg is by no means unique. Neither is he typical, since union representatives' work often varies, even at the same location. But there are constants; and a look at Mr. Bragg's work along the Wixom assembly line helps to clarify some of the issues underlying the current negotiations.

Foot-Soldier at Work

To some extent, the content of Mr. Bragg's work on a typical day is deceptive. While his fellow workers spend their time monotonously piecing together over 300 cars, their union representative seems to spend much of his time roaming around, slapping people on the back, chit-chatting and poking his head into unfinished cars to check things out. But it's all done for a purpose: finding problems.

"The main function of a committeeman is to settle problems right on the floor," Mr. Bragg says. "I'm a mediator, a foot-soldier out there. Without the committeemen, Ford couldn't run this plant."

Ford might dispute this assertion, but there is no denying that Mr. Bragg's meanderings uncover problems—or that he is the man on the spot. For while Mr. Woodcock and other union leaders are making speeches on such lofty topics as "dignity in the work place" or "shared decision-making," it is Charlie Bragg and the men like him who are fighting disciplinary actions, getting supply-racks fixed, arranging days off, getting bathrooms cleaned and drinking fountains unclogged. (On an average day, Mr. Bragg handles about 20 individual problems.)

In the course of attacking such problems, Mr. Bragg avoids threats and confrontations. His prime goal, he says, is keeping his constituents happy. But he also must remain on working terms with their supervisors, who, he feels, must regard him as tough, but flexible. Indeed, he uses his ultimate weapon—the formal, written grievance—sparingly; and he says he tries hardest to avert, rather than win, disciplinary cases.

"A grievance can just lie around for weeks," he says. "Meanwhile, the problem might be corrected anyway. What I want to do is take care of the problem—and do it quickly."

Keeping Cool

Take the case of the open ceiling vent that was blowing a draft of cool air on some workers. When informed of the problem, Mr. Bragg relayed it to the foreman whose "zone" was affected. Hours later, when he returned to the zone to find the vent still open, Mr. Bragg didn't yell. Nor did he write a health-and-safety grievance. Instead, he simply picked up the foreman's phone—in the foreman's presence—and called the necessary people. The vent was soon closed.

"You can get more by trying to find ways to get things done than by screaming," Mr. Bragg says.

Health and safety disputes—such as the vent problem—are serious business at Ford. Not only have they historically been a key factor in local strikes, but now, under new federal laws, they are subject to intervention by government inspectors. In fact, so anxious is the company to resolve them quickly that it issues a weekly list at Wixom of unresolved grievances in this area and meets weekly with the union to clear them up.

But crucial or not, health and safety problems must be sandwiched in among a wide variety of other activities in Charlie Bragg's day. Recently, for example, within the span of a few hours, he got a man's pay adjusted upwards, arranged for the reinstatement of a fired worker and saw that new tools were issued to two other workers. Then, later in the same day, he managed to get a planned disciplinary action against a worker dropped by convincing the man's supervisors that discipline would accomplish nothing. (The worker had stamped 19 cars with wrong serial numbers; the error, Mr. Bragg maintained, was inadvertent.)

Then there is the problem of "standards" grievances. According to Mr. Bragg, these complaints—centered on the detailed definition of jobs on the line—supersede even health and safety problems as the toughest issue he must face. "Standards men are running our plant, and it's killing us," Mr. Bragg asserts. "In the old days, you had time to go to the bathroom if you wanted. Now, you need a relief man for that. You can't even breathe. These standards experts went to school, but they don't take the human factor into account."

Mr. Bragg maintains that Ford is constantly trying to slash the allowed time and boost the required work for each job. Ford disputes this claim. Nevertheless, Mr. Bragg and the other committeemen carry stopwatches for the purpose of timing each assembly-line zone in their districts. If the speed is too high, they complain. (Conversely, however, Mr. Bragg kept quiet on one recent occasion when the line was moving too slowly.)

Restructuring a Procedure

The committeemen also fight for workers who believe their jobs contain too many steps to fit the available time. Mr. Bragg, for example, recently handled such a complaint from a veteran worker assigned to put trim pieces on car doors. Timing the man, Mr. Bragg found that only 1.2 seconds were allowed for errors and tool changes between cars. Ford disputed the figure but finally agreed to delete a step from the job.

Such standards problems intensify several times a year, when line speeds or model mixtures are altered to conform with market conditions. Complaints soar during these periods, Mr. Bragg says. "Those are the times you wish you didn't have this job," he says. "You wish you could just crawl in a hole and hide."

But the standards problem isn't a headache only for the committeemen, Mr. Bragg insists. Eventually, he feels, it results in the bane of a plant manager's life: worker absenteeism. "These tight standards and the heavy compulsory overtime cause a lot of the absenteeism," Mr. Bragg says. "It's like a spider web to people. They're so tired when they get home, they can't even mow the lawn. So they miss the next day."

One solution to this impasse, Mr. Bragg believes, is the voluntary overtime proposal being advanced by UAW leaders in the current negotiations. He also likes another proposal by some UAW leaders to offer bonus vacation days to workers with good attendance records. Such workers, he says, currently receive nothing "but a hard time when they finally do need a day off."

Unpopular Decisions

This isn't to say that Charlie Bragg believes his workers are always right. Indeed, on some occasions, he says, he is forced to make politically unpopular decisions. "I'm not afraid to tell a man when he's wrong," he says. "There's no sense fighting a fruitless battle. It just creates more problems."

That policy can have painful consequences, though, as Mr. Bragg discovered earlier this year. His only election opponent for the committeeman's position, he says, ran against him because of just such a case. "He was working a job installing back-window trim," Mr. Bragg recalls. "He said he didn't have enough time to do it, but I timed him, and he did. When I told him, he accused me of not doing my job."

Mr. Bragg generally tries to avoid such a contretemps by compromise. But in some cases, when this seems impossible between the principals involved, he tries other tactics—one of these being the ploy of playing one manager against another. For example, on one occasion he went all the way to the plant management level to get an unpaid leave for a man who wanted to go to Italy to get married.

"Most of my job is just common sense," Charlie Bragg says. But common sense doesn't always triumph, and Charlie Bragg doesn't always get his way. Recently, in fact, he lost two discipline cases in a row, both concerning absenteeism. Although he had tried to refute company records and had argued against tough penalties for the men, their records were poor. The most he could accomplish was to get their penalties reduced to probation—a temporary solution at best.

Leave It to Charlie

Another disappointment came when a carefully arranged compromise in a tough case dissolved because the worker involved decided to take things into his own hands. The man, a chronic absentee case, had suddenly been switched out of a choice job to one that was clearly less desirable. His foreman contended the move resulted from the man's attendance record; but the worker called Mr. Bragg in to complain that the switch was really a retaliation because he had left early one day to take his wife home from the hospital.

Mr. Bragg carefully arranged a face-saving compromise in which the man would have been switched back to his old job on the understanding that he, Mr. Bragg, would counsel the worker and persuade him to mend his ways. But the arrangement was wrecked when the worker, before he learned of management's reversal, staged a one-man strike on his new job.

Mr. Bragg, furious, berated the worker, but the issue was dead and the man returned to the less desired post.

Problems such as these, Mr. Bragg feels, wouldn't arise in the first place if there weren't bad foremen. "A bad foreman," he says, "is a guy who doesn't care about his people. All he cares about is just trying to get that dollar, and he lets his bosses or his employes run his area. He's inconsistent. He lets things run rampant for a while then tries to crack down all at once without being fair. Nobody respects him."

The real mark of a bad foreman, Mr. Bragg says, is to shunt work onto the shoulders of committeemen. In a case not long ago, he says, a foreman insisted that it was the committeeman's job to intervene in a feud between two workers—a job, Mr. Bragg asserts, that is properly that of the foreman. Nevertheless, he says, "the committeeman is finding himself more and more doing a foreman's work, because they say they're too busy, and they know we'll do it for the people."

A High Profile

On the other hand, Mr. Bragg admits, there are bad committeemen—men who write grievances simply to get workers off their backs or who wait until six months before an election to clear up long-overdue problems. To avoid these pitfalls, Mr. Bragg says that he makes it a point to follow up all requests as soon as possible and to be constantly available. "The natural thing," Mr. Bragg says, "is for people to wonder, 'What's that son of a gun doing for me?' I try to make sure they see me every day so they know."

Mr. Bragg's vote-getting appeal—he won the last election by a six-to-one margin—indicates that his workers believe he is doing something for them. "He's an outstanding committeeman," says one. "He comes around and talks to you, and when he's paged, he'll make it there as quick as he can. . . . He'll win some for you and he'll lose some, but the losses are always close." (The Wixom foremen also seem to respect Mr. Bragg—although their praise isn't always unqualified. "He's one of the better commiteemen," says one, Ed Hendrix, "even though he and I don't get along." Mr. Hendrix adds: "He's on his side of the fence, and I'm on mine.")

If Mr. Bragg is the model of the confident committeeman these days, it wasn't always that way. In late 1970, when the president of his local union asked Mr. Bragg, then a repair worker and alternate committeeman, to step into a vacated post of a departed committeeman, he wasn't sure he could do the job. "But everybody helped me," he recalls, "and I picked it up pretty fast."

For his efforts as a committeeman, Mr. Bragg earns about $14,000 a year (the same as he would be earning as a repairman); and during his 16 years at Wixom he and his wife (who used to work) have been able to save enough to afford a three-bedroom house, a swimming pool, a pickup-truck camper, and three Honda motorcycles—one for Mr. Bragg himself and one each for the Braggs' two sons, aged 17 and 15. In addition, the family has a red 1969 Pontiac Catalina which Mr. Bragg drives to work at Ford. (Why doesn't he drive a Ford car? "I like Pontiacs," he says.)

Mr. Bragg spends some time as a volunteer fireman and an active member of the Masons. He used to coach Little League baseball and play golf weekly, but he has had to give up those activities because of the time and pressure of his union post. This time and pressure worries his wife, Sally, the high school sweetheart whom he married after graduation in 1955. "She's proud of my being a committeeman," Mr. Bragg says, "but she also says it's too time-demanding. She says it's wearing on me. I don't see it, but she does."

Indeed, Charlie Bragg likes his job so well that he is already planning to run in 1975 for another two-year term. What's more, he says he isn't tempted by offers he has had to become a foreman. "I just don't feel comfortable in a white shirt and tie," he says.

ON THE LINE - II

By Laurence G. O'Donnell
Staff Reporter of The Wall Street Journal

WIXOM, Mich.—When two workers on the giant assembly line at the Ford Motor Co. plant here were recently assigned some extra work, a war of nerves ensued. The workers, who balked at the tasks, had trouble keeping up with the pace of the line and called in their union representative to protest the situation. The union man argued that the workload was too heavy. But a company official, who makes time studies, insisted that there was plenty of time because the line speed had been slowed.

The hassle went on for several days, with experts from the union and the company continuing their bickering. The workers continued to protest. Then, in the face of threatened discipline, the workers backed down. A full-fledged crisis had been averted.

It was then, and only then, that Ed Hendrix breathed a sigh of relief. Mr. Hendrix is a foreman in charge of a 300-foot stretch of the Wixom assembly line, and, as such, he is very much the man in the middle in such crisis-threatening disputes. As Ford's man on the spot, it is up to Mr. Hendrix to battle the union, please his bosses and keep the pressure on his workers so that the company's Thunderbirds and Mark IVs will keep rolling off the line. And even after disputes are finally settled, and the union and top company officials have long forgotten the details, it is Mr. Hendrix who often must live with the consequential bitter feelings.

"The foreman is the punching bag," the 29-year-old Mr. Hendrix says. "You get your ears beat off from both sides of the fence."

But such are the facts of life for Ed Hendrix and the rest of the 8,000 or so assembly-line foremen in the 44 huge auto factories scattered across the country. They are men who are caught in the center of a system of tight discipline and relentless pressure—a system upon which the auto companies rely to keep the lines moving day and night, five or six days a week.

Bored Workers

The system is getting harder and harder to maintain. Given the choice, many—perhaps most—workers on auto assembly lines would rather avoid the mechanical, repetitive tasks that constitute their jobs. "You do this 250 to 350 times a day," says a bushy-haired young man screwing control panels to car doors. "It isn't a hard job. Just boring as hell." In fact, problems and complaints about the system are behind many of the issues currently being raised by the United Auto Workers Union in its local and national bargaining with Ford, General Motors Corp. and Chrysler Corp.

The particulars of a foreman's job vary plant by plant and line by line. There are numerous generalities, however; and some time spent with Ed Hendrix in Ford's Wixom plant help to clarify many of the main points being stressed in the industry's latest negotiations.

The pressure on Ed Hendrix begins and ends with management's desire to achieve maximum production and profit without sacrificing quality. Specifically, Mr. Hendrix feels the pressure—indeed he expects it—from several sources: the general foreman, who is his immediate boss; the superintendent of his department, who can promote him —or fire him; other foremen, whose own workers are affected by the output of Mr. Hendrix' men; and the two inspectors who oversee his "zone."

But Ed Hendrix also applies his own pressure. "I drift along the line," he says. "I check the installations. If there is a problem, I talk to the operator." And he accepts no excuses from his workers. If prodding doesn't work, he calls in the union man. If discipline is necessary, he applies it. Yet he seems careful to always seek a balance—pushing hard enough to get the work done, but never so hard that he'll incur backlash from his men and the union.

Limited Power

Mr. Hendrix well understands the limits of his powers over his men. ("It's easy to make a foreman look bad," says one of his workers. "Just screw up.") Although as a foreman he can prod and discipline, he can't fire, transfer or even grant a worker a day off for personal business without clearing it with someone higher up. What's more, the union representative with whom Mr. Hendrix deals can go over the foreman's head—and often does—with the result that some of Mr. Hendrix's decisions are overturned. "It happens," the foreman says. "No committeeman likes to see his man get disciplined."

One reason for a foreman's constant watchfulness is that hundreds of things can go wrong during an average day. There is the constant danger of industrial accidents. Workers may be absent, or late, or leave early without permission. Or they many run out of parts, a particularly crucial problem. On a recent occasion, for example, Mr. Hendrix himself ran to get some missing parts, even though he was risking a contract violation because the rules say foremen aren't supposed to do physical work. And, more often than not, one crisis will lead to another—an accident can lead to a worker shortage, which can lead to a supply problem.

And all the while, car after car after car goes by, for only in extreme emergencies does Mr. Hendrix hit a button and stop the line. He tries to avoid that action at all costs, explaining that it means idling 1,600 workers up and down the line—at $5 an hour each. Consequently, during his five years as a foreman, Mr. Hendrix has hit the button only a few times—preferring where possible to have workers chase after cars.

Nevertheless, Ed Hendrix is considered a better-than-average foreman by the men under his supervision. "He's reasonable and fair, and that's all I expect of a guy," says Tim Schoening, a worker in Mr. Hendrix's zone. Says another worker: "If you do your job, he leaves you alone."

Indeed, Mr. Hendrix says he tries not to get too close to his workers (one reason his home phone is unlisted). "I don't drink with them very often," he says. "Sometimes it is hard to be a friend and a foreman." And while he does talk to his workers while on the job, it is mostly about their parts supply and their tools. "I used to be scared of the men," he says. "But after a while, you get a thick skin. When you come through the door, you say, 'I've got a job to do. They've got a job to do.' You get so you can look 'em square in the eye."

That he does. For example, when a worker has trouble installing a screw and wants to skip it, Mr. Hendrix says: "That's a lot of crap. You don't walk to the next car as far as I'm concerned." Nor does he tolerate sloppiness, such as a worker leaving extra screws in the cars. "A penny a piece. That adds up," he says.

Potential for Advancement

It is instincts like these that Ford admires and that have helped Mr. Hendrix shine in the eyes of C. Van Snyder, his superintendent. Mr. Snyder has 19 foremen working for him, five of whom, he says, are "moving around because they show potential for advancement." Ed Hendrix is one of the five.

Despite his progress the pressure still seems to get to Mr. Hendrix. He smokes constantly. He drinks black coffee all day long. When the line stops at 4:30 p.m., he can't click it off in his mind. "I carry it home," he says. "Some nights I don't sleep at all, worrying about where I'm going to get the men (the next morning). I let my wife listen to me. Sometimes I take it out on the kids." And he still wonders whether his job is secure. "You feel they may come down here and fire you because you can't run your own area," he says.

The shifts at the Wixom plant vary in length from eight to ten hours, depending on activity. When Mr. Hendrix works the day turn (he switches shifts every four months), he sometimes must get up as early as 4 a.m. and then doesn't get home again until 5:30 or 6 p.m.—usually dog-tired.

"Maybe one night a week I'll hit the rack at 8:30 or nine to catch up on my sleep," Mr. Hendrix says, adding that he was so tired driving home one Saturday this year that he fell asleep and collided with another car.

The Lure of Money

With all the disadvantages, why be a foreman? The answer at least for Mr. Hendrix, is money. His current salary is about $13,000 a year, several thousand dollars more than he would make as an hourly worker. He also picked up an extra $5,000 over the past year from overtime, boosting his total annual income to more than $18,000.

He needs this money, Mr. Hendrix says. He has a sick daughter, which prevents his wife from working and has resulted in a pile of medical bills. Furthermore, the Hendrixes like the possessions they can afford on a foreman's pay—part interest in a camper, a second car, two hunting dogs, a snowmobile, a new motorcycle.

But another reason that Ed Hendrix became a foreman was the chance to escape the line and become a part of management. "It was boring, stagnant, I wasn't creating anything," he says of his first job in an auto plant (as a paint sprayer for GM). Later he got a job as an inspector at the Wixom plant and was subsequently offered a chance to become a foreman.

"I felt I wasn't trained for it," says Mr. Hendrix, who is a high school graduate. But, he recalls, "they said they'd help me." Training consisted of one week's instruction (Ford requires two weeks now). However, Mr. Hendrix says that experience has been his best educator and that life as a foreman "never worked the way" the instructor said it would.

One thing a foreman soon learns is that no two days are exactly alike, yet there is a certain sameness that permeates Mr. Hendrix's working life. For most of the first hour of most days, he grapples with manpower problems. He needs 34 people to run his area and has a pool of four to six workers to tap when workers are missing. These days, he usually needs all the workers in the pool, and occasionally he needs even more than that.

"The Men Are Tired"

The manpower problem has been exacerbated in recent months, Mr. Hendrix says, because the long hours that constitute his people's workday have contributed to doubling plant absenteeism over the last year to recent levels in excess of 10%. "The men are tired of it," Mr. Hendrix says. "They spend too much time away from home." But he doesn't condone absenteeism, however logical the cause. "It causes all our other problems," he says. "When absenteeism is high, that's when I lose quality."

His zone runs smoothest, of course, when he has his work slots filled with trained people. To maintain quality on days when trained workers are missing, he sometimes has to assign two substitutes to one job—one to keep track of the parts, the other to do the actual work—and then explain later why he exceeded his budgeted manpower. But on some Mondays, the manpower shortage becomes so acute that the plant closes down a half-hour in the morning and another half-hour in the afternoon so that the workers can get the six minutes an hour of relief time specified in their contract.

How should unexcused absenteeism be dealt with? Sternly, Mr. Hendrix believes; indeed if he had his way, he'd impose a one-day disciplinary layoff for unexcused absences. The current system, which starts with 12 minutes off without pay, is "much too slow," he asserts.

Working within the rules, Mr. Hendrix nevertheless tries to be tough, calling an "AWOL" to his desk the morning the man returns to work. "I talk to him about why he was absent," Mr. Hendrix says, after which he says he calls the labor relations department to check the man's record. If the worker has missed one or two days, the foreman calls the union. "I have the committeeman talk to him to tell him he is heading for a disciplinary layoff," Mr. Hendrix says.

In one typical recent case, he planned to be tough with Rick, a 19-year-old installer of rear-window molding who had missed two days in a row and had been disciplined only a month earlier. In a hearing in the superintendent's office, Mr. Hendrix laid out his case against the pony-tailed worker, who seemed unimpressed by the proceedings. "They (company officials) do what they want anyhow," Rick grumbled at one point.

The union representative defended the worker, arguing that a disciplinary layoff wouldn't help to change Rick's attitude. In fact, even Mr. Snyder, the superintendent, seemed to think Rick should get another chance. And so, feeling somewhat undercut, Mr. Hendrix pocketed the discipline—an 18-minute penalty—but nevertheless kept in the back of his mind that the penalty could be served later in case of a further infraction.

Later, Mr. Hendrix said he had originally planned to tell the worker to take the rest of the day off without pay. But he didn't take this action when he learned during the hearing that the union official and the superintendent were friends of Rick's father, who also works in the plant. Then, too, Mr. Hendrix said, layoffs deprive the foreman of a trained worker; and because of the physically taxing nature of Rick's work—involving climbing in and out of cars— "it would take three days to train a man for the job and even then he wouldn't be real good."

To help cut absenteeism, the UAW is asking the auto companies in this summer's bargaining for a change in the overtime rules, making overtime work voluntary instead of compulsory. The union's theory is that voluntary overtime would ease the pressure of the long hours and the resulting urge to take days off. Foreman Hendrix, however, doesn't think much of the plan. "It would hurt me. You have to have trained operators," he says. "If 14 guys said, 'I don't want to work,' I'd be hurting."

Mr. Hendrix says his zone also suffers from contract abuses. For example, under the contract he isn't allowed to refuse any worker permission to go to the plant medical clinic; however, he says that some workers take advantage of this provision to shirk their jobs. But on their part, some of Mr. Hendrix's workers claim that he is paranoid on the subject of contract abuses. "He thinks everyone is out to screw him," one worker says. "He dreams some of it up. He wouldn't talk to one girl after she took a medical leave even though they used to talk and buy each other coffee."

In any case, Ed Hendrix feels that his workers might do well to follow his own example. During the past year, he says, he missed only one day—when there were two feet of snow on the ground. He adds that he would have been fetched at home by plant guards in a four-wheel-drive truck if other workers hadn't been absent in such numbers that the plant eventually had to close down. But a foreman's life being what it is, Mr. Hendrix says that he was later called on the carpet for being absent.

EDGY EMPLOYES

By Lewis M. Phelps
Staff Reporter of The Wall Street Journal

Workers are responding to the economic slump by piling a record number of grievances on management's doorstep.

That's the view of men on both sides of the bargaining table as more companies seek to bolster sagging profits by tightening operations. Layoffs and cost-cutting drives are running smack into union efforts to keep their members working and earning enough money to cope with continuing inflation.

Observers of the labor-management scene note that worker complaints about the application of their labor contracts always rise when the economy turns sour; the last peak in grievance filings came during the slowdown of 1966. But though precise figures are lacking, they almost unanimously assert that the present situation is the worst within memory.

"I've had more grievances dumped on my desk in the past two months than I had all last year," says an official of a large United Auto Workers union local in Detroit. The veteran labor relations manager for an Eastern manufacturing company comments: "We've got more disputes going here than the United Nations."

Foreshadowing Contract Demands

The current spate of grievances is more than just a minor headache for firms. Because so many of them are tied to the vital question of who works and who doesn't, unions are pushing them with extraordinary vigor. According to the Federal Mediation and Conciliation Service, which provides arbitration services in some hard-to-resolve grievance disputes, requests for grievance arbitration in the fiscal year ending June 30 should exceed 10,000, about 20% more than in fiscal 1969. A grievance that goes all the way to arbitration can involve hundreds of hours of work and cost both management and unions thousands of dollars.

In addition, the type of grievances unions file often provides a clue to what they'll ask when contract time comes. Unions have stressed higher pay in most recent bargaining rounds, but there are indications that the emphasis might start to swing to job security in the months ahead.

I. W. Abel, president of the United Steelworkers union, said recently that pressure was building in his union for such goals as a shorter workweek and other forms of layoff protection. When unemployment rises as it has been doing, "you get people thinking more about sharing the available work," said Mr. Abel, who next year will head USW bargainers in the talks on new labor contracts for some 550,000 workers in the can, aluminum and basic steel industries.

"Bumping" New Workers

For now, the main thrust of union grievances has been to keep older, more senior workers on the job. This is in keeping with unions' long-held principle that the first workers hired should be the last fired in bad times. When layoffs come, high-seniority employes in departments touched by the ax often try to keep working by "bumping" less senior people from other jobs. The rub comes when the company takes the position that the senior man can't adequately perform the job he wants to take over.

A case in point occurred recently at White Motor Corp. in Cleveland. A laid-off sales department worker with 29 years' seniority sought to bump a more junior tax department clerk. The company let the older employe try out for the job but after five days decided he couldn't do it. The worker's union, a UAW local, filed a grievance, claiming that five days wasn't long enough to learn the new tasks.

The matter was resolved when the senior worker's sales department job was reinstated, but resolution of a similar problem at a West Coast aerospace firm wasn't nearly as easy. There, the union attempted to displace five inspectors of a spacecraft subassembly with higher-seniority men who had been laid off from assembly line jobs. After several months of wrangling, the firm compromised by agreeing to train two of the laid-off employes for inspector posts. "It took three months to train them and it cost us thousands of dollars," grumbles a company official.

Blowing the Whistle

Unions are trying to preserve the jobs of junior as well as senior members by insisting that companies follow to the letter the detailed job descriptions that are part of most labor contracts. Thus, at McDonnell Douglas Corp. in St. Louis the International Association of Machinists successfully launched a grievance when the company tried to order maintenance men to do work normally assigned to painters. And at one large auto plant the UAW squawked when a foreman was caught removing a misassembled auto body from a production line.

The auto company involved claims that the situation was an emergency that called for prompt action, and a UAW man privately concedes "that probably was the case." But he continues: "In times like these you blow the whistle on any little thing. If you let them get away with something like that once, pretty soon the foremen will be doing more and more, and our guys will be laid off."

Much the same philosophy applies when companies attempt to introduce cost-cutting techniques at a time when layoffs are widespread. Firms are being hit more frequently with union grievances alleging production line "speedups." The usual company response to such charges is a simple denial, and union men admit that the claim often is hard to prove. But this hasn't stopped them from making it.

Says a union shop steward in one Chicago plant: "A foreman with a fast monkey wrench can speed up a line quite a bit. It's a constant battle you have to fight, and it's gotten much worse lately."

Even management moves not expressly designed to speed production have been the cause of trouble lately. Several months ago International Harvester Co. installed a computerized monitoring system to improve maintenance scheduling in its Chicago truck assembly plant. But workers feared it would also be used to check the efficiency of assembly line workers. When a grievance on the issue moved slowly, the workers struck. Harvester got them back after two days by signing an agreement that it wouldn't give time-and-motion study experts access to the computer.

Workers also are using the grievance procedure to try to put a few extra dollars in their paychecks. In good times they do this by claiming they aren't getting their share of overtime work; in a slump they must be more inventive.

In the basic steel industry company officials say they are being besieged with grievances from workers who want to benefit from incentive pay bonuses. "Our men seem to be finding guys on incentives in other plants with jobs similar to theirs, so they think they should get it. too," says an Inland Steel Co. executive.

THE FINAL WORD

By ELLIOT CARLSON
Staff Reporter of THE WALL STREET JOURNAL

NEW YORK—The chauffeured car jerks to a halt and Eric Schmertz hops out—dapper, quick-stepping, a lithe figure in herringbone heading a flying wedge of lawyers who tumble out after him. The wedge bears down upon the headquarters of a local cab company and its unsuspecting manager, standing outside.

"We're innocent," the manager cries, playfully raising his hands into the air. But Eric Schmertz has no time for banter. He and his entourage sweep into the front office, asking questions, requesting records, looking the place over.

Obviously, Mr. Schmertz isn't on a social call. One of the nation's busiest labor arbitrators, he's doing one of the things he enjoys most: checking to see if an arbitration decision he handed down is being obeyed. It doesn't take long. A look at washroom facilities and a check on work practices that once stirred bitter quarrels convinces him that, for the moment, all is well. Abruptly, the group is moving again—homing in on another unsuspecting cab company.

"Dropping in this way you see conditions as they are," explains Mr. Schmertz. "They don't have time to arrange things just for you." Besides, he adds, "I like getting out of cloistered offices."

Who's That on the Firetruck?

Eric Schmertz is constantly getting out—and to the bottom of things. To understand labor wrangles, he has ridden firetrucks in Harlem, strode the halls of a hospital emergency ward, sat in the cockpit of a two-engine trainer aircraft. For Mr. Schmertz believes in getting a feel for his work. It is one of the traits that make him a different kind of arbitrator—and, some believe, a prototype of the arbitrator of the future.

What arbitrators think, and do, is bound to profoundly affect U.S. labor relations. No longer are arbitrators used only occasionally, or by just a few industries. Today, anxious to avert strikes and long court fights, disputants are turning to them more than ever to resolve contract wrangles. And as public employe unionization spreads, arbitrators are sure to be called on even more, even to the extent of settling terms of new contracts rather than just interpreting old ones.

At this very time, though, arbitrators are torn between two contrasting codes of professional behavior. In a field still dominated by a shrinking band of aging men, the traditionalist code holds that an arbitrator should be almost as cloistered as a judge—aloof, majestically impartial, limiting himself strictly to the narrowest possible interpretation of the problem at hand.

Arbitrators "often get too close to the parties and thus risk losing their impartiality," grumbles Philip Carey, a longtime New York pro. "So they shouldn't try to be nice guys or do-gooders—just umpires."

A Man in the Middle

At the other extreme are Mr. Carey's nice guys and do-gooders, mostly younger men who take a decidedly activist approach to their profession. They think arbitrators should be a force for good, as they define it. They contend that an arbitrator's ruling should always square with equal hiring laws and other social reform legislation—even when the dispute at hand could be settled strictly on the contract.

Carefully picking his way between these two poles is Eric Schmertz, who has some ideas of his own.

Though insisting that arbitrators' authority should be kept limited, he nonetheless asserts that many veterans view their jobs too narrowly. He'd like to see them leave the cloister for the firetruck occasionally, tempering their legal knowledge with a feel for various jobs and the labor-management problems they generate. He bids his colleagues to be more flexible, to play a greater variety of roles. Specifically, he urges his fellow arbitrators to do less arbitrating and more mediating, a role they've historically shunned.

Some experts predict the Schmertz approach will prevail. "Eric is a kind of model of what future arbitrators will be like," says Robert Coulson, president of the American Arbitration Association, a nonprofit group that supplies arbitrators. There is sure to be greater demand for arbitrators who, like Mr. Schmertz, "take into account all the factors affecting an industry" yet do so without exceeding their limited authority under labor contracts, he says.

Artful and Not Overbearing

Despite their wide differences in philosophy, most arbitrators go about the job of arbitrating in much the same way. Gritty, stubborn, often a little theatrical, they like being the boss and work hard at keeping control of arbitration proceedings. A good many of those proceedings begin in the small hearing rooms atop the skyscraper here housing the American Arbitration Association. Many courtroom rules apply as the arbitrator listens to both sides, taking notes or having them recorded by court reporters.

Enjoying informality, Mr. Schmertz prefers to work without the usual judicial trappings and takes the notes himself. Yet he maintains order by demonstrating what he calls "a kind of sophisticated authority." "You've got to be artful," observes the graying, scholarly Mr. Schmertz. "Arbitrators who are overbearing get nowhere."

Sitting in his big swivel chair, taking testimony from a cab driver who has lodged a grievance, Mr. Schmertz is indeed both suave and tough. The cabby feels wronged. His commission on fares has been cut to 42% from 50%. But his boss is in the hearing room, too, defending the change. The driver quit for a time and then returned, agreeing to be accepted as a new employe, the boss argues. New cabbies aren't entitled to the higher rate.

The cabby launches into a tirade, voice quivering, face reddening, ready to leap out of his chair. "Frenchie," he shouts, "cleared it with Heinie. . . ." It is a truly impassioned performance. But who is Frenchie? And who is Heinie? Whoever they are, neither they nor the cabby's testimony thus far has much bearing on the issue at hand.

So Mr. Schmertz assumes a mock judicial air and cuts the cabbie off in a half-humorous, half scolding way. The tension drains away, and the hearing gets back on the track.

(Mr. Schmertz later ruled for the cabby, on the ground that he had no right under the contract to make this kind of private deal—coming back as a new employe—with his employer.)

The hearing over, Mr. Schmertz, followed by union and industry lawyers, jumps into the chauffeured car to inspect cab company garages. Upon arrival, he maneuvers through grease-spattered work areas without getting so much as a smudge on his best herringbone suit, moving the way one might expect of a onetime college second-baseman. (He was once offered a contract with the Pittsburgh Pirates. "I rejected it," he says, "deciding I'd always be in the minors.")

And he makes sure his orders are being carried out; they require, among other things, that owners provide drivers with clean toilet facilities. Exerting control—this is when Eric Schmertz seems happiest. "It's satisfying seeing your decisions actually taking hold," he says.

But Mr. Schmertz holds there are times when a simple arbitration award will do little to assure labor peace. On these occasions, he suggests arbitrators seek permission to mediate and strive for voluntary, long-range solutions.

Case of the Overworked Firemen

How Mr. Schmertz moves in and out of these various roles is illustrated by his performance in a firemen's case. Originally, the parties wanted a simple ruling on whether New York's firemen were overworked. He could have ruled—and settled the matter for a while —on the basis of facts from a single grievance. But hoping for a lasting solution, Mr. Schmertz sought a broader mandate: permission to devise, for the first time, standards for measuring workloads. The parties agreed.

So after weeks of fact-finding, including a stint in a Harlem firehouse, he came up with a complex formula under which firemen get lots of points for fighting large fires and a lesser number for fighting smaller ones. A station is deemed undermanned if a certain point total is exceeded.

The system is still new. Some labor-management experts suspect it's too complicated and won't work, and both parties involved remain wary of it. "Nobody has figured it out yet," says Frank Palumbo, vice president of the Uniformed Firefighters Association of New York City.

Mr. Schmertz' style is as controversial as some of his solutions. One fellow arbitrator calls the firetruck riding and other acts of derring-do "gimmickry." But Mr. Schmertz insists he's really a "strict constructionist" in his handling of cases. And, indeed, a conservative approach is evident in those cases where the parties rule out one of his experimental mediation efforts and require that he simply arbitrate in the old way.

A Conservative Approach

Then Mr. Schmertz, unlike the young activists in his profession, limits himself to deciding whether one of the parties has breached the contract. He worries very little about fairness or civil-rights laws—just enforcement of the contract.

In one recent case, Mr. Schmertz heard a widow's plea for vacation money from her deceased husband's employer, on the ground it would have been due had the husband lived. Mr. Schmertz ruled she was entitled to the money, even though the employer had granted her husband a six-month leave of absence at full pay to recover from a heart attack. He explained that the firm hadn't made its generous leave conditional on surrender of vacation rights provided by the contract.

There always has to be a loser, however, and some parties hate losing more than others. This also makes life hard for the arbitrator, whose judgment is often questioned no matter what his philosophy. Mr. Schmertz finds himself in such a situation right now. Recently, three Teamster union locals filed a motion in federal court in Newark, N.J., to set aside one of Mr. Schmertz' arbitration awards on the ground of nondisclosure of certain pertinent data.

The locals are protesting Mr. Schmertz' decision that P. Ballantine & Sons, which in March sold its brewery assets to the Falstaff Brewing Corp., had no obligation to continue pension contributions to an industry-wide fund once the concern was out of business. The unions contend the June 14 award should be vacated because neither the arbitrator nor Ballantine disclosed to all the parties that Mr. Schmertz' cousin, Robert Schmertz, was allegedly negotiating with Ballantine and its parent, Investors Funding Corp., for the acquisition of the Boston Celtics basketball team, which Ballantine owned.

Mr. Schmertz and his cousin deny any impropriety or that any such talks were going on during the time Eric Schmertz was arbitrating the case. In fact, Eric Schmertz claims he didn't know that Ballantine even owned the team or that his cousin might, at some point, be interested in buying it.

Whatever the outcome of the case, it illustrates the growing controversy over the strict constructionist philosophy of arbitration. One union lawyer argues that Eric Schmertz failed to give sufficient weight to the plight of the workers who, for no fault of their own, will lose further pension contributions from Ballantine. Eric Schmertz agrees this is too bad but insists that, under the contract, Ballantine was obligated to contribute to the pension fund only for "compensable" days actually worked by Ballantine employes. And with Ballantine's ex-employes no longer working "compensable" days, this obligation is at an end, the arbitrator says.

"It isn't my job to tell the parties what's right or wrong," says Mr. Schmertz. "It's simply my role to tell the parties what they can do inside the contract they negotiated. They don't want constitutional lectures on whether their contract contains inequities."

Most old pros concur. But the younger practitioners claim this very philosophy is what's wrong with arbitration today. They contend that arbitrators frequently invite court challenges, and costly delay, by ignoring civil-rights laws and guidelines on hiring minorities when they write their decisions.

The young activists want arbitrators to be more lenient on blacks in some discharge cases and, occasionally, to actually help promote minority-group members even when the contract, perhaps in violation of federal hiring guidelines, specifically provides for lines of progression that favor whites. "It's irresponsible for arbitrators to render awards that contradict the law, even when they're consistent with the contracts," says one.

Mr. Schmertz disagrees. If arbitrators were to rule on matters not intended by the parties, he argues, it would undermine their acceptability in the future. And, he adds, there already are too few arbitrators with wide acceptability for that to be permitted.

Nearly 95% of all contracts now provide for arbitration of squabbles arising from them, and the Arbitration Association's caseload jumped to 6,658 last year from 4,007 as recently as 1966. But there aren't enough new arbitrators gaining acceptance to keep up with demand, and the mainstays keep getting older. The average age of arbitrators has risen to 57 from 50 since 1952; last year, arbitrators over 60 made about 42% of the awards in cases handled through the association.

The problem is that most disputants would rather rely upon an aging prima donna than take a chance on an unknown. This makes it hard for a new face to get established. But 46-year-old Mr. Schmertz, a comparative newcomer, is that rarity, someone who brought to the field a familiar name and a reputation for impartiality when he entered private practice in 1962. This was due, in part, to his service for several years as director of the New York State Board of Mediation. And bolstering his image as a neutral was his previous experience on both sides of the street—as a union organizer and corporate personnel man.

Now Mr. Schmertz, one of about 1,300 people on a national list from which arbitrators can be drawn, has more work than he can handle. Indeed, he's booked up solid with arbitration hearings for the next three months, a typical wait for a top arbitrator. Nor do his services come cheap. He charges $200 for the usual one day of hearing on a case and $200 for each day of study. But like others, he charges the full daily fee whether or not a full day of work is actually required, and he can often handle more than one case in a day.

All of which makes his work profitable. Of the $130,000 he earned last year, $95,000 came from arbitrating about 200 cases. The remainder came from a teaching job at Hofstra University's law school and his post as a public member of the New York City Office of Collective Bargaining.

Arbitration may be profitable, but it's also perilous. In one case handled by another arbitrator, a brawling worker lunged across a table, fists clenched, after the arbitrator upheld the worker's discharge for unruliness. The man had to be pinned down while the arbitrator made his getaway.

Even more harrowing was the experience of a New York arbitrator asked to rule on a work slowdown by a union noted for its toughness. Unhappy with the way the hearing was going, several unionists grabbed the man and led him to a 17th-floor window. They gave him two choices: rule favorably or get thrown through the window.

The arbitrator resigned on the spot.

THE WORKER'S VOICE

By Neil Ulman
Staff Reporter of The Wall Street Journal.

DUSSELDORF, West Germany—Suppose the president of U.S. Steel couldn't name the man he wanted to head the company's top subsidiary because workers elected to the board of directors didn't like his candidate.

Or suppose management had to absorb six months of continuing losses at another subsidiary because worker directors wouldn't agree to close it. Or suppose the company couldn't switch production from one subsidiary to another because workers didn't approve.

A preposterous nightmare for U.S. Steel, perhaps. But nothing more than the facts of industrial life for two big German companies in recent months. In one, the redoubtable House of Krupp, the worker directors' balkiness was partly responsible for the resignation of the president, Jurgen Krackow, after only three months in office.

None of the cases, however, represented a super display of union economic power. Workers' rights to be represented in varying strength on all public companies' "supervisory" boards are guaranteed by law in Germany. The system has been around since World War II, and it has been gradually strengthened over the years with new legislation, including big additions to workers' rights that went into effect last year.

A Common Market Model?

And now the Common Market Commission has proposed that all "European-chartered companies" in the newly expanded nine-nation market accept as a model the German system of workers' voice in management.

The Netherlands has long used a similar system, and late last year Norway adopted a law very close to the German model. Such facts lend weight to the opinion of one management consultant here that "this thing is going to spread gradually throughout Europe no matter what the Common Market ministers decide." Thus, American companies that incorporate subsidiaries in the future under a European charter or even national law could find themselves facing a whole new set of labor-relations rules.

All of which may sound scary to managers but needn't be, at least not for a while, say businessmen who have dealt with the German system. For one thing, in most cases the shareholder-elected directors have a two-to-one numerical advantage over the worker directors, so the latter can easily be outvoted. But management men worry because unions are pushing for equal representation on the boards. Such parity already exists in the coal and steel industries and has caused some problems there, officials say.

Some Advantages Also

But while most industry officials worry about the day that parity arrives, they believe they can live with the present system and even see some advantages to it.

"My advice to Americans dealing with the German labor law for the first time is don't have it read by an American lawyer. He's likely to go into a state of shock followed by panic," says John MacDonald, a management consultant in the Dusseldorf office of McKinsey & Co. "The wording of the law sounds terribly tough. But it usually works out quite reasonably in practice."

The second bit of advice to Americans from

Mr. MacDonald and others on both the labor and management sides in Germany is to familiarize themselves with the broad outlines of all German company-organization and labor law before trying to understand elements out of context.

The key to that law—and the part that the Common Market Commission wants to spread throughout the community—lies in the "two-tier board." Under the most common application of this system, the annual shareholder meeting elects two-thirds of the members of the senior, or supervisory, board. The other third are elected by the company's workers. The supervisory board, in turn, appoints the management board, which actually runs the company. Members of the supervisory board cannot belong to the management board or vice versa. The supervisory board meets four or five times a year, passes on major investments or structural changes, and approves accounts. But it is restrained by law from interfering in day-to-day management.

The Works Council

Because German labor unions bargain on a regional, industry-wide basis rather than company by company, that leaves a large area of concern to workers in individual enterprises up to still another institution, the works council.

All workers in a firm with five or more employes are entitled to elect a works council, which may range from three members to 50. Members and officials of a council needn't belong to the union but usually do. They have broad rights to be kept informed by management of all developments that could affect employes' jobs. For instance, an industry-wide contract might cover only pay and hours. Within the framework of that pact, an individual works council might have equal voice with management on such matters as hiring and firing, shifting jobs, and starting and quitting times. In the U.S., these details might be covered by local plant bargaining or simply left to management; the union must use its economic power to bargain for a say. In Germany, the works council by law is guaranteed a voice.

The Common Market's proposed European company law would incorporate the two-tier board with at least one-third of the supervisory board elected by a company's works council.

Having worker directors make up one-third of the supervisory board "is a wonderful thing; nothing could be better. You should do that in your country as soon as possible," Andreas Kleffel, a director of Germany's powerful Deutsche Bank, tells an American visitor. Mr. Kleffel sits on 14 supervisory boards and is

chairman of two major German companies, Hapag-Lloyd, a travel and shipping firm, and Rheinstahl, a diversified steelmaker.

Mr. Kleffel credits this system as being the main reason for Germany's record of relative labor peace over the last 20 years, compared with the labor disputes in Britain, France and Italy. The effect, he says, is that "labor people come onto a board with the idea that they are going to teach management a thing or two and set matters straight. But when they have to look at all the company's problems, see the financial figures and participate in decisions, it changes their attitude."

In addition, Mr. Kleffel says, worker directors often provide wise and effective counsel. He cites the example of a firm in which half the stock was closely held by two members of the management board who had an argument serious enough to reach the supervisory board he headed.

One of the men became so incensed that he threatened to throw his shares on the market and enlist the public in the battle against the other. Then, Mr. Kleffel says, one of the company's oldest worker directors spoke up: "We have known you for a long time," he told his "boss," whom he was legally empowered to advise and control. "Surely you wouldn't do a damn fool thing like that and lose face with all of us."

The result was sudden and enduring silence, Mr. Kleffel says. "We heard no more about it. It was a wonderful remark but one that I could never have made," he says.

But there is a simpler reason why Mr. Kleffel and other businessmen find favor with one-third worker representation on boards. "There aren't any problems with this system," Mr. Kleffel says, "because the workers haven't any real power to force their views. When the workers' advice is good, it is listened to." Otherwise, the shareholders' directors vote them down.

For example, at Ford-Werke in Cologne, Ford Motor Co.'s German subsidiary, the two worker directors on the six-man supervisory board almost always call for cutting the dividend and either plowing the funds back into the company or paying them out in higher wages and benefits for the workers. What happens? "Nothing," a member of Ford's management says with a shrug. "Four-to-two. That's the vote, and that's the end of it."

Ernst Lueck, the 39-year-old chairman of Ford-Werke's central plant council and a member of the supervisory board, also shrugs. On investment of profits, he says, "I don't get anywhere. I'm in the minority. We state our point of view, but we always lose the vote."

Even Horst Bergemann, Ford's director of labor relations, says the presence of worker directors on the supervisory board doesn't much influence him, even though the supervisory board must vote to appoint him. "They are in a minority," he says; "they haven't any power."

"Constant Discussion"

Of more concern to Mr. Bergemann is the 12-member works council, with which he meets monthly. Its powers have been augmented by a law passed last summer. "In the past," Mr. Bergemann says, "when we wanted to hire someone, we just did it and told the works council later. All they had was a right of information. Now we tell them beforehand and get their consent. They don't withhold consent in practice, but it means constant discussion back and forth about why we're hiring someone instead of promoting from within and that sort of thing."

The works council must also give its consent to overtime and has a right to participate in decisions on who will be selected for training and who will be hired to train them. "A majority" of works-council requests involving additional costs or benefits are turned down, Mr. Bergemann says. But the council, in effect, retains a veto power over all company initiatives affecting jobs. "The most important thing is keeping the workers informed," Mr. Bergemann says. "If you explain why you want to do things, they usually go along."

Thus, despite the increased powers of the works councils, most managers are happy under the German system provided they have a "reasonable" council and a two-thirds majority in the supervisory board. "But all this may change in the near future," Mr. Bergemann says, referring to labor-union political pressure to give parity to workers on supervisory boards in all companies. "This could change our way of life completely, though we're really not sure how," he says.

"A Bad Thing"

Mr. Kleffel, the director of Deutsche Bank, thinks he knows. In the German coal and steel industry, where parity exists already, "It gets to be a bad thing. . . . The workers' side has real power," he says. Thus, the Confederation of German Employers Associations is bitterly opposed to extending parity throughout industry. But many believe it is coming—sooner or later. "My bet would be that we'll have a definite trend toward parity in the next two or three years," says Prof. Kurt Biedenkopf, a director of Henkel & Co., chairman of the Biedenkopf Commission on German labor law and an adviser on labor to the Common Market Commission.

Under the system as it currently operates in the coal and steel industry, supervisory boards are composed of 11 or 21 members. Of an 11-man board, five are elected by the shareholders and five by the workers; of a 21-man board, it is 10 and 10. The 11th or 21st member is called the "neutral man." But Mr. Kleffel says: "The worker directors will only agree to a man who has their confidence. They are normally professors or politicians of leftist persuasion," though a popular one has often been Hermann J. Abs, chairman of Deutsche Bank, who enjoys a good reputation with labor. Of course, the "neutral man" presumably also enjoys the confidence of the shareholders' directors, who wouldn't otherwise vote for him.

What management finds most distasteful about parity is the potentially high degree of worker control over investment. If workers at Ford-Werke, for example, really could cut the dividend and force the company to apply the funds elsewhere, it could do "quite some harm," Mr. Bergemann asserts. "A lot of unions couldn't care less about economic questions. We fear they would use board positions just to further their political aims," he says, echoing a theme frequently expressed by German management.

German workers naturally don't think there is any "harm" in diverting a larger share of funds from investment to wages and benefits. "You have capital on one side, the workers on the other side and the company in between," says Mr. Lueck, who is on Ford-Werke's supervisory board. As he sees it, "each side wants to take out as much for itself as possible. But both sides want the enterprise to succeed."

As for injecting national politics into the boardroom, some worker directors do feel that they "represent the interest of labor in Germany as a whole" in the boardroom, according to Gerhard Leminski, who edits a trade-union magazine and sits on the board of Fried. Krupp Huettenwerke. "That's an abstraction, admittedly," that can lead to conflicts of interest, he says.

Mr. Kleffel, the businessman, cites the case of a big steelmaker on whose board he sits that had to face the problem of a foundry that was "losing money at a high rate." The plant "was in deplorable conditions, and there was a clear decision by management to close it and fix a severance payment for the workers," Mr. Kleffel says. However, he adds, the 21st man on the supervisory board was a Social Democratic Party politician who came under pressure from party members in the foundry area.

So the board kept putting off the decision while he appeased his political following with plans to seek new orders for the foundry. "No amount of orders could have kept it going; it was just inefficient and uneconomical," Mr. Kleffel says. Finally, after three supervisory-board meetings, two special commission meetings and six months of additional heavy losses, the foundry was closed, he says.

In the case of Mr. Krackow, his rapid demise at Krupp can be laid at least partly to worker directors refusal to accept his nominee to head the company's biggest steelmaking subsidiary, Fried. Krupp Huettenwerke. The supervisory board still hasn't agreed on a candidate, although Mr. Krackow has long been gone. Shareholders and worker directors have "agreed to cooperate constructively on choosing a man," says Gerhard Leminski. They just haven't found the man yet, he says, adding, "It's a very complicated situation."

BY THE BOOK

By Richard F. Janssen
Staff Reporter of The Wall Street Journal

FRANKFURT—It was high noon at the airport where everything appeared to be going in Germany's characteristic style of orderly hedonism. The jets were setting down regularly from a cloudless sky, and passengers were browsing quietly through the unabashed gadgetry of the airport sex shop. Behind the scenes, the air-traffic controllers were letting their eyes flit between their glowing green radar screens and their neatly folded newspapers.

In the navigation office, Karl M. Heinlein appeared to be concentrating on conversation. But appearances can be deceiving. He had been glancing furtively at his wristwatch, and he interrupted with obvious displeasure: "The last 10 departures were at 2½-minute intervals."

That's only 30 seconds more than the normal maximum here. But if it were kept up all day, the cumulative effect would become costly in terms of schedule delays at airports around the world, squandered fuel, canceled flights, passenger irritation, perhaps pilot fatigue and thus even safety, Mr. Heinlein complained.

Such delays, in fact, were deliberately kept up all the way from late May through late November as Germany's controllers staged a "work-to-rule." Their aim was to win wage increases and other benefits of the sort conventionally sought by a strike. "But this isn't a strike," protested Walter Achenbach, a black-bearded, 37-year-old controller. "What we are doing are just things prescribed in our rule book."

An Increasingly Common Tactic

The technique of putting bargaining pressure on management by zealous—or overzealous—adherence to the formal rules laid down for various jobs is becoming increasingly common in Europe and Japan. It is especially well-established in England, where railmen resorted to the tactic again yesterday morning to back up pay demands.

The approach is little known in the U.S., but that could change because working-to-rule offers labor one big advantage: "If the workers go on strike, their wages are cut off for the duration, but with a work-to-rule they keep on collecting their regular paychecks," a European labor expert says. Union headquarters benefit, too, because the dues keep flowing in, and they needn't dip into strike funds (usually leaner than in the U.S.).

"A quest for better ways to resolve labor disputes" without the widespread hardship caused by all-out strikes is under way in many nations, the New York-based Conference Board notes, and unions are clearly interested. "We're working on a whole new series of actions short of strikes that have the same effect," says Charles Levinson, secretary general of the Geneva-based International Federation of Chemical and General Workers Unions, which is linked with major U.S. unions.

Even if the practice doesn't spread swiftly to the U.S., it is already affecting the overseas units of American multinational companies. And it appears particularly well-tailored for employes in the swelling public sectors of the U.S. and other industrial nations; in these sectors, traditional strikes are often outlawed, and governments have laid down volumes of rules to assure that work is done properly and safely.

That is the situation with the air-traffic controllers in Germany, where the rule book requires that they maintain a horizontal separation of not less than three miles between planes within 30 miles of their radar antenna at Frankfurt. "Two miles are just as safe as three miles if you're 100% certain" that the planes actually are two miles apart, Mr. Achenbach asserts. Normally, he says, the controllers will take it "on our own necks" to permit lesser separations and thus avoid congestion.

But to be absolutely sure that no plane violates the minimum three-mile rule, Mr. Achenbach reasons, it is possible for controllers to instruct pilots to strive for "a five- or six-mile separation."

They were "following the rules closely," concedes Mr. Heinlein, the controllers' boss. But they were "not using their skills" by applying the rules with their usual flexibility, he complains. Because so much must be left to the judgment of the controllers, the managers are helpless against a careful work-to-rule. If a controller were caught ordering 60-minute intervals between departures, "I could fire him," Mr. Heinlein says. But going from two minutes to four minutes would be far from clear-cut evidence of incompetence, he says.

Before their action was suspended (on the German government's promise of a fair deal and its plea to stop wasting scarce fuel), the controllers made their mark in a number of ways. The delays of up to three hours "made it impossible for me to make a rendezvous after a flight," a Swissair stewardess complains. Lufthansa lost nearly $90 million, the German airline figures, mainly because of flight cancellations. Many travelers tried to bypass Germany, and the government found that deliberate delay of just one Munich-to-Cologne flight cost an extra 20,200 gallons of fuel.

Unclear Origins

The origins of working-to-rule aren't altogether clear, but it is widely agreed that the practice took firm root in England soon after World War II. "We call it the English disease," a West German industrialist says. As to why it didn't start sooner, a Continental expert explains, "Unions are like people—sometimes they get smarter as they mature."

A leading British practitioner of the art agrees. An all-out strike would cost his union about $72,000 a day in strike benefits, explains Ray Buckton, general secretary of the Associated Society of Locomotive Engineers and Firemen. That would make up only a fraction of the regular pay lost by the 29,500 members, he notes, and a total stoppage also "hurts your kith and kin" because members of other unions are laid off or can't get to work.

"The last thing this union wants to do is strike," he asserts. Except for scattered 24-hour walkouts, the union hasn't staged a full-scale strike since 1955 (it lasted 17 days). That isn't because it bargains with a delicacy befitting the outlying Victorian mansion that is its headquarters (the still-elegant meeting hall was once Sir Thomas Beecham's music room). Rather, it is that experience shows management "is hurt far more" by working-to-rule than by a closedown, Mr. Buckton declares.

Current Issue: Speedometers

Rigid adherence to even a single rule can cause "a tremendous inconvenience," Mr. Buckton says. Thousands of London-area commuters concur. Many trains now are being canceled because union members are refusing to take out trains lacking the full safety equipment required by rules. Currently, the issue is speedometers; management concedes that many older locomotives have never been fitted out with them.

"If everybody strictly adhered to all the rules in the book, the railroad would grind to a halt," Mr. Buckton contends, adding that rigid adherence to even a single rule can cause "a tremendous inconvenience." Usually, for instance, a crew will cut short its lunch or "physical-needs break" to get a late-arriving train out again on schedule. But during a work-to-rule, he adds, a crewman will say, "Hell, no, I'm taking my full 30 minutes"; delays start accumulating all through the system.

The classic case of the British trainmen's tactics is one that causes Mr. Buckton to chuckle and brings grudging admiration from officials of the nationalized British Railways Board. Their rule book specifies that a member of the train crew "must see that the doors of the carriages and other vehicles are properly closed and fastened and must assist the station staff in closing them."

Typically, a crewman complies in a matter of seconds by merely glancing back out the window of the cab, seeing by the uniform horizontal angle of the door handles that all the doors are closed, union and management men agree. But during a work-to-rule, they say, he will leave the cab, walk slowly along both sides of the entire train and examine each door handle. There are 20 doors on each passenger car, so the process can take almost as long as the crewman wants.

The Cooperative Spirit

As commonplace as the term work-to-rule is

in European newspapers, there is some grumbling about the semantics on both sides. "It is a misnomer, it really means going slow," a British rail spokesman says. He contends that it amounts to "overzealous adherence to the letter of the law" instead of its spirit. The term prompts foreigners to worry that it is unsafe to ride British trains during normal times when the rules presumably are being ignored, says Mr. Buckton, who much prefers the term "non-cooperation."

With a little imagination, working-to-rule can be effective even in factories that lack highly detailed rules but depend on a cooperative spirit "Working-to-rule is only doing what you get paid for, when in actual fact, we do a lot more," says a bespectacled lathe turner in England's industrial north. At his plant, he explains, the rules require someone else to bring him a basket containing all the plans, parts and tools he needs.

But often an item or two are missing, so he will round them up himself. If the union there decides on the work-to-rule it is considering, he explains, he would insist on waiting for everything to be brought to him. With everyone else taking the same stance, he figures, there could easily be "a two- or three-hour delay" before the harried helper could provide everything. "If everybody only did what he was paid to do, just imagine the confusion," he says.

"Obviously, we'd rather have a work-to-rule anytime" than go on strike, says Jack Ashmore, the sandy-haired local union leader at Padley & Venables Ltd., a Sheffield, England, subsidiary of Gardner-Denver Co., Quincy, Ill. The British unit has recently undergone two weeks of working-to-rule. "It's more of an economic threat to the company" than a strike, he asserts, reasoning that the company's overhead costs continue while production drops off.

In British manufacturing, both sides appear to find the burden sharing relatively tolerable. A company's customers aren't completely cut off from their supplies, so future business is less likely to be lost to competitors. A prolonged strike in a labor-scarce economy would risk mass defections of skilled workers to other employers, management sources say. And union leaders believe that their influence is greater when men stay at work than when a strike sends them scattering to fishing spots or temporary jobs.